Adios to the Brushlands

A WARDLAW BOOK

Adios to the Brushlands

Arturo Longoria

TEXAS A&M UNIVERSITY PRESS
COLLEGE STATION

Second Printing, 2016

The paper used in this book meets the minimum requirements of the American National Standard for Permanence of Paper for Printed Library Materials, Z39.48-1984. Binding materials have been chosen for durability.
∞

Library of Congress Cataloging-in-Publication Data

Longoria, Arturo, 1948–
Adios to the brushlands / Arturo Longoria. — 1st ed.
p. cm. — (A Wardlaw book)
Includes bibliographical references.
1. Shrubland ecology—Texas, South. 2. Nature conservation—Texas, South. 3. Longoria, Arturo, 1948– . I. Title. II. Series.
QH105.T4L65 1997 97-14541
333.75—dc21 CIP

ISBN 13: 978-0-89096-769-0 (cloth)
ISBN 13: 978-1-62349-486-5 (paper)
ISBN 13: 978-1-62349-487-2 (ebook)

For Norma

And for

Nomar, Jason,

Matthew, & Ethan

Contents

Publisher's Acknowledgment

Texas A&M University Press is privileged to add its imprint to this Wardlaw Book. The designation claims a special place in the list of Texas A&M publications.

Supported with funds inspired by the initiative of Chester Kerr, former head of Yale University Press, this book and its companion volumes perpetuate the association of Frank H. Wardlaw's name with a select group of titles appropriate to his reputation as man of letters, distinguished publisher, and founder of three university presses.

Donors of these funds represent a wide cross section of Frank Wardlaw's admirers, including colleagues from scholarly presses throughout the country as well as those from other callings who recognize and applaud the many contributions that he has made to scholarship, literature, and publishing in his four decades of active service.

Texas A&M University Press acknowledges with profound appreciation these donors.

Mr. Herbert S. Bailey, Jr.
Mr. Robert Barnes
Mr. W. Walker Cowen
Mr. Robert S. Davis
Mr. John Ervin, Jr.
Mr. William D. Fitch
Mr. August Frugé
Mr. David H. Gilbert
Mr. Kenneth Johnson
Mr. Chester Kerr
Mr. Robert T. King
Mr. Carl C. Krueger, Jr.
Mr. John H. Kyle
John and Sara Lindsey
Mrs. S. M. McAshan, Jr.
Mr. Kenneth E. Montague
Mr. Edward J. Mosher
Mrs. Florence Rosengren
Mr. Jack Schulman
Mr. C. B. Smith
Mr. Richard A. Smith
Mr. Stanley Sommers
Dr. Frank E. Vandiver
Ms. Maud E. Wilcox
Mr. John Williams

Their bounty has assured that Wardlaw Books will be a special source of instruction and entertainment to the reading public for many years to come.

Preface

This book is neither a scientific treatise on the habitats of South Texas nor a concise history of the region. It is, quite simply, the chronicle of one man's life in the Brushlands. Besides, as too often happens, science—when economic benefits are at hand—has become less empirical than political. And history, as well, has evolved into an allegory (an invention) designed to buttress the few at the expense of the many.

I am not attempting to win friends, though I must admit that I *am* trying to influence people. Unfortunately, when words skip too closely to the truth, and when economic and political powers are threatened, facts and truths become as imperiled as those sons and daughters of nature who have sought no economic scheme by which to survive. I therefore present a simple and honest appraisal of the Brushlands; and the only gain I have received in these many years was a filling of my heart.

I want to thank the people who allowed me to interview them over the years, and whose knowledge of various South Texas Brushland subjects helped to create this book. I'd also like to thank the editors of *Texas Parks & Wildlife* and *Texas Highways* magazines who helped me hone my writing skills and allowed me to indulge in the subjects I love. Special thanks also go to those who reviewed the text and provided excellent advice on how to make the message clearer.

Adios to the Brushlands

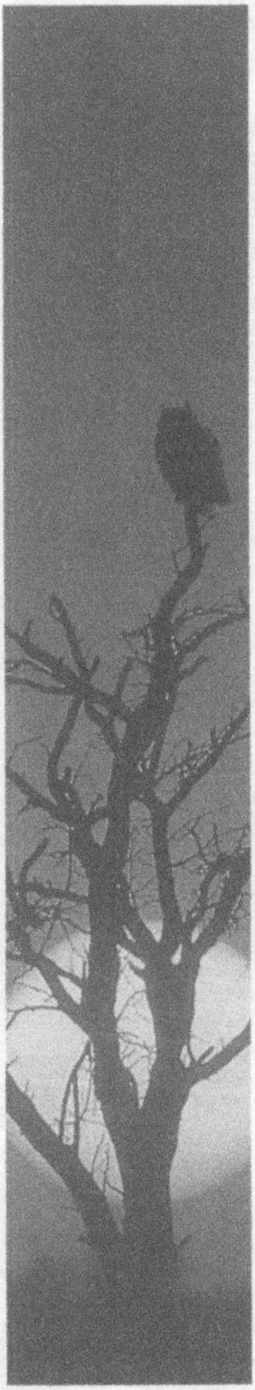

Part I
Beginnings

I HAVE A FRIEND who says that love for the Brushlands evolves after being exposed to it through things like hunting and bird watching. For some, perhaps, that might be true. But for me it was different. Since childhood, the brush itself—*thick, briary, and still*—has been the breath of my life. Yes, I have hunted, and I have spent many hours watching birds, studying reptiles, and identifying plants. But confined to a preserve or zoo, those endeavors would hold little interest. It was always the brush with its collage of shrubs, trees, and cacti that possessed and nursed me. The brush, for me, offered the simplest of loves, profound and undying in its effect. It drew out of me fears and feelings of hopelessness. In subtle ways it was a teacher as well as a sanctuary, offering me the spiritual awareness that on occasion I have so desperately desired.

From boyhood to middle age, I have found the Brushlands of deep South Texas and northern Mexico a special friend; a day spent away from the chaparral is for me a day lost. Some will not understand; even those who are born in the Brushlands sometimes never connect with it. I was lucky.

When I was boy, growing up in the town of Mission, the Brushlands were still vast; machines had yet to devour the upland areas surrounding McCook, or the hills north of Rio Grande City, or the thickets that enveloped San Isidro.

My old friend Mario Hernandez and I spent many hot summer afternoons and frigid winter mornings wandering through the brush. On weekends, during the school year, we would accompany my grandfather, Papagrande, to El Ponderosita—the ninety-acre ranchito northeast of La Joya that belonged to my Uncle Bill. There was a small brick cabin there that Papagrande, Uncle Bill, and Uncle Trini had built.

But perhaps I should backtrack a bit. It is in northern Mexico that the story really begins . . .

El Cuervo

My father, Ramon J. Longoria, purchased a ranch twenty miles east of San Fernando, Tamaulipas, Mexico, in 1959. He called it *El Cuervo.*

The ranch—a montage of thickly wooded hills and steep gullies—stretched north from the lethargic San Fernando River for seven miles.

I first visited El Cuervo in the summer of 1959 during the time when my father was having a stone-walled cabin built on a hill that overlooked the San Fernando. We camped beneath a simple *portal:* four *barretta* trunks stripped of limbs and leaves and held in place by small limestone boulders, on which structure was placed a mat of grass and dried twigs to provide an anemic shade.

Though I was no stranger to the brush, when I awoke on that first morning—a pink sun emerging from behind a monolithic plateau in the east—and I saw the thick stands of barretta trees braced stoically on a surreal stage, the sky and clouds painted on a soft canvas behind it, I felt for the first time that feeling of awe and adventure that was to carry me, wrapped within its leafy blanket, through life.

Mine was not the ghetto story—the child raised in the barrio, the farmworker's son, the Mexican immigrant overcoming the challenges of a new land. I was raised speaking English, the son of a fifth-generation Texan father and a Texas-born mother whose parents had fled to the United States when revolution swept Mexico.

I was the progeny of ranch people. For them, life's epicenter was not any specific language or country but instead *el monte,* that untamed woods of twisted trees and briary shrubs from which warmth and sustenance, and other blessed gifts emerged. My father's father had driven horses from Edinburg to San Antonio in the days when pronghorn antelope still roamed the eolian sands and oak motts of northern Brooks County, and mesquite and nopal lay across Hidalgo and Starr counties like wool on an unshorn lamb. My mother's father, too, had spent his life close to the brush, raising his children in a house on an almost forgotten road, four miles from a nearly forgotten town in northern Starr County.

So what if El Cuervo was in Mexico? The country in which it lay was of no importance. It was simply an extension of the brush that rose from the foothills south of the Mexican town of Jimenez along the banks of El Rio Soto la Marina and sprawled north, crossing the great Rio Grande until it dissolved amidst the mountain laurels, oaks, and pecans of the Texas Hill Country at the Nueces River. The land remained unaware of the concept of boundary lines; borders are the projects of politicians and bureaucrats, and El Cuervo and all the brush that surrounded it could never be truly possessed. They could only be understood. But understanding comes from growth, and growth evolves from exposure. What exists as foreign and wild in the beginning becomes natural and tranquil within the subtle revelations of nature. Tenuous at first, that path reveals itself not by way of its gentle contours but from the very obstacles and deterrents that border it.

One moonless and cloudless summer's night the ranch foreman, Don Teodoro, came to my father and said that a cow was lost. He said we should go to an isolated spot on the ranch and listen. He said the cow wore a bell that could be heard from a great distance. Squatting on a gravelly road, embraced by penetrating quiet and bathed by the radiance from a million stars that gathered in clusters and streams and stretched from horizon to horizon like luminous dust and sparkling pebbles, we waited.

Don Teodoro and my father spoke in low, nearly hushed tones. I assume they were discussing cattle and such, but I could hear only the phonetic melody of their voices. Why it came to mind, I cannot recall, but I realized at that moment that without my father there to protect me, I could never have sat on that lonely road, surrounded by the unknown, listening patiently for the gossamer clang of a wooden clapper on a brass bell. It was okay as long as Dad was with me. I the child, he the father: one who was afraid but found solace through his parent, the other undoubtedly experiencing fear but deriving appeasement from within.

In the distance, a mockingbird volunteered a fusillade of falsetto sounds, mimicking the avian calls of the region. And now and then a solitary coyote cried out, searching for a mate, or a friend.

"Ay esta," Don Teodoro mumbled, his finger pointing slowly in the direction of the faraway sound that coalesced into a feeble clang. *"Mañana entramos con los caballos."*

We walked carefully back to the pickup, always watching for the rattlesnakes that might lie coiled on the warm road bed. Tomorrow, Don Teodoro and his *vaqueros* would ride in the direction from which the bell had sounded and return the lost cow to the herd. But all I could think of was how I treasured those fleeting moments with my father.

• • •

El Cuervo was where I first ventured into the woods alone. At the time I did not consider it a milestone. But things would never be quite the same after that. The absolute trust I had placed in my father to protect me was now, in some nebulous way, transferred to me.

The transference came, as it often does, without fanfare. One morning I simply grabbed the Savage .30-30 bolt rifle kept handy at the stone-walled cabin and I walked into manhood. The year was 1962, or thereabouts. It was late spring; the leaves were wet with dew and freshly green. The trail I chose was dense with foliage, overgrown and obscure—a preamble of the life to come, perhaps. It was also the day I discovered the great benefits of woods roaming.

Woods roaming is more than mere walking. It is a form of meditation, a way to the intrinsic self. It allows one to see conceptually. It reveals. But it is not a form of physical exercise, though undoubtedly the soma benefits. Woods roaming is a state of mind.

The .30-30 I carried that day was a crutch: a long arm reaching back to my father, protecting me in the uncharted maze that lay ahead. Like a yearling deer, I stepped cautiously, unwilling to blunder headlong into the unknown.

I walked unhurried, dewy-wet from the knees down, reveling in my solitude. I saw as I had never seen before. Now I alone would provide for my safety. I heard everything—the raspy whistle of a scaled quail, the snapping flutter of large, green grasshoppers, the swaying of ancient barretta limbs.

As I walked a strange energy began coursing through me, filling me with sensations that, until then, I had never known. I studied the trees—the speckled-white barretta, the crenulated bark of massive black ebonies, the smooth emerald limbs of palo verde, the mottled gray branches of the brasil—all the while a gentle breeze fluttering across leaves sparkling green and gray, and tempting me onward.

Midway through the walk, I spotted a chachalaca perched on the limb of a Mexican olive tree. Since that first summer when Dad built the stone cabin, I had heard chachalacas many times. At daybreak their galloping calls echoed up from the San Fernando River like trumpets stuck on a staccato cadence. But now was the first time I had seen a chachalaca up close. The bird stared at me, I stared back—a long moment—restless brown eyes winking and shifting, one spindly leg held up, nape feathers flared. I stepped back. With determined wing thrusts the bird was gone, lost in a mesh of thorns and branches.

As I walked farther, time passed of its own accord; the sun marking its endless journey overhead; the morphology of burgeoning clouds and waning shadows bathing the land in hues too numerous to recount. At last, I sauntered up to the stone cabin having followed the rocky wash that crept down the hill on the northwest side. I was thirsty and hungry. The gathering clouds seemed to reinforce the feelings of tranquility that ushered me along, that had filtered up from the earth in a delicate osmosis working its way through my body like an ethereal mist. I stepped into the cabin, having been gone but a couple of hours, yet at the same time having transcended one stage of my life to enter another.

In early fall, we caught butterflies in wire-rimmed mist nets that were fashioned into large socks. There were millions of butterflies at El Cuervo. I spent hours trying to match my specimens with the pictures in the field manual, *Butterflies of North America.*

Mostly, however, the fall was reserved for hunting. El Cuervo was where I shot my first deer: a fat doe that appeared one foggy morning a hundred yards down a *sendero* that Petroleos Mexicanos (Mexico's national oil company) had cut through the brush. Dad heard the boom of the .270 rifle clear back at the cabin. When he arrived I was too nervous to join in the search, so he and Don Teodoro went looking for the deer. Dad found it; the animal had traveled only a few yards.

Another milestone. A father's proud smile. The young brave could now feed the camp.

Then there was New Year's Eve of 1965. Dad had brought me to El Cuervo deer hunting. A frigid norther had blown through, and we hadn't bathed in several days. We slept in the sheet-metal-roofed brick lean-to that braced the stone cabin's north side, because though cool in the summer, the cabin's high thatch roof allowed heat to escape in the winter. A cramped ten by twenty feet, the lean-to served as kitchen and dining room. And on that cold New Year's night, it was the only place to keep warm.

Windows shut tightly, a glowing propane flame issuing from the blackened burners in the corner, I huddled in one sleeping bag and Dad ensconced in another, shared laughter helping us ignore the ripe smell of feet gone unwashed.

On hot summer days I would sit atop the water tank on the west side of the stone cabin. From that vantage place—some ten feet above the highest point on the hill—I could see plainly the blue mountains to the west, which we called the Victoria Mountains. Sometimes I would sit for hours, watching turkey vultures climb invisible thermals, listening to the soft cooing of white-tipped doves, and gazing at the mosaic of greens that rippled into the distance. Something told me that I should swallow every angstrom of this beauty, commit it to memory, and hold it firmly in my heart. It was an education that might someday serve me well.

On lazy afternoons I would follow the trails that paralleled the slothful San Fernando. I'd find a spot on the cool, damp earth—places where the river was no more than fifty yards across, and where tall trees hunched over the water's edge like old men—and observe the dark green current as it reluctantly inched its way to the coast. Now and then a group of *cuervos* (the crows from which the ranch got its name) would fly over me, screaming hoarsely *mari, mari, mari,* as if it were a blasphemy. I shot a few crows. I was young and ignorant.

Occasionally, my cousins would accompany us to El Cuervo. The first thing they wanted to do was ride horses. I could not see the fascination. There was no direct contact with the earth. Besides, the horses made too much noise. They scared animals away. They could only traverse well-marked trails—never *through* the brush, never up steep banks or down narrow ravines. Sometimes horses had minds of their own. I swore I'd never ride atop anything that could think for itself.

I'd let my cousins mount their steeds and go their way, talking loudly, silhouetted against the bright sun, trot noises reverberating into the woods like rimfire rounds shot from a pistol. It didn't occur to them to whisper; they never learned to tiptoe lightly; they weren't interested in watching birds or lizards or deer.

I was unprepared for my last visit to El Cuervo. In retrospect, I imagine it was just another prelude to so many instances in later life where no proper goodbyes were said, the assumption being that there would always be another day.

That final journey came during the Easter vacation in 1967. It was supposed to be a three-day trip. It turned into a one-day tour. By then Dad had become a wheeler-dealer businessman, too busy to enjoy the brush. I was into varmint calling at the time. I wanted to try my calling skills at the ranch. Because Mexican soldiers operating along the roadways often confiscated guns, even when permits had been issued, we hid a Remington model 600 .222 rifle and a pouch full of calls—Burnham, Herters, Olts—in the Jeep Wagoneer and headed south. We arrived at El Cuervo in the early morning. I roamed the lazy trails as I had done so many times before. By late afternoon, I'd collected two bobcats. I enjoyed the hunt, but the real treat was to be at the ranch, and with Dad. I looked forward to a couple of nights in the stone cabin, its straw roof layered over the vaulted rafters, cool Gulf air steering the sounds of pauraques and screech owls through the windows. But it wasn't to be. As we watched one of the vaqueros skin out the cats, Dad said: "Let's head home. You've shot a couple of bobcats—that should do it."

I don't remember what I said, if anything at all. We loaded the Jeep and that was that. Dad sold the ranch a few months later because the Mexican agrarians were threatening to take it away—by force if need be.

But the memories persist. Now, when I am in one of my sunken, teary moods, I sometimes close my eyes and find myself sitting on the old water tank next to the stone cabin. I look west at the far-off mountains, and I hear the white-tipped doves, their soft coos filtering from the barretta woods. I watch the turkey vultures flying high overhead, and I smell the clean air. For a long, wishful moment, I sit on that old, red water tank, remembering. It was an education indeed.

El Ponderosita

My learning continued at the place we called *El Ponderosita,* a small ranchito, just thirty acres in the beginning. My mother's brother, Bill Valverde, bought the land in 1960. Located fifteen miles northwest of Mission, it bristled with native habitat that reached deep into the infinity of innocent eyes. Old mesquite and ebony trees graced the earth with their slumberous shade; and filling the voids beneath them were solitary shrubs and clumps of spiny cactus.

Crown of thorns, cenizo, granjeno, nopal, uña de gato, pitaya, Mormon tea, lote bush, retama, chaparro prieto, huisachillo, pencil cactus, salvia, guajillo, horse crippler, coma (erroneously called la coma), fishhook cactus, alicoche cactus, pincushion cactus, anacahuita, tasajillo, ocote, palo verde, coyotillo, brasil, yucca, guayacan, and scores of other shrubs and small trees—a large percentage of them legumes, almost all with thorns and each perfectly suited for its particular niche in Brushland ecology—stood in stalwart tranquility.

Concealed within were white-tailed deer, javelina, coyotes, bobcats, raccoons, ocelots, weasels, opossums, badgers, gray foxes, ground squirrels, cottontail rabbits, jaguarundis, skunks, kangaroo mice, field rats, and shrews. And diamondback rattlesnakes, indigo snakes, rat snakes, corn snakes, coral snakes, bull snakes, hog-nosed snakes, cat-eyed snakes, garter snakes, blind snakes. And countless lizards, skinks, and frogs. Critters small and large, nocturnal, diurnal, crepuscular, walking and sliding, barking, howling, hissing—all of them beneath a raucous umbrella of calls and whistles from hundreds of birds that hopped from branches to pads and nested among protective thorns. These were the Brushlands of my youth.

My education followed a circuitous route. Each season disclosed its own subtle dictates, for the woods were a place of nourishment—for body as well as soul. I was fortunate that my grandfather was there to guide me. Under his tutelage the woods and I became one.

Papagrande was what we called my grandfather. His real name was Trinidad Marcos Valverde, Sr. He gave El Ponderosita its name—a takeoff from the television show *Bonanza.* In many ways the ranchito belonged to him. The thirty acres that eventually grew into ninety were the joy of Papagrande's later years. He never worried that old age might sneak up on him while he was alone in the brush. If it did, then that was okay: *"Es un buen lugar para morir."*

The late afternoon walk was what both of us looked forward to. Thin trails weaving between the arthritic limbs of ancient mesquites, circling clumps of red-flowered prickly pear cactus, then edging motts of emerald-leafed coma and gray-leafed purple sage; the diaphanous fragrance of yellow huisache flowers whiffing through the air; the sky etched with chalky clouds; Papagrande leading, I ambling behind. *Silence.* Each step placed carefully, avoiding brittle sticks, sidestepping thorns and spines, eyes intent on the ground but always aware of the skyline. Papagrande gesturing at the tracks of a deer or javelina, then examining the diminutive nest of a blue-gray gnatcatcher. *"Cuidado con las viboras,"* he would whisper, as he indicated a clump of dry grass.

In the early years El Ponderosita was maggoty with rattlesnakes. Often we would see three or four in one afternoon, sometimes as many as ten. But in those days the brush lay everywhere, and the vipers had plenty of food. For each snake there were two or three packrat nests, and at night the kangaroo mice would amuse us as they hopped in front of our vehicle's headlights—their long tails etching tiny grooves in the sandy soil, their front legs tucked degeneratively next to their plump bodies.

A respect for rattlesnakes forced us to abandon our early camp under the stars. A couple of years after he purchased El Ponderosita, Uncle Bill—along with his younger brother, Uncle Trini, and Papagrande—built a small brick cabin with a connecting pipe-framed porch. That become headquarters: the Valverde family's meeting place for barbecues, poker games, and for listening to professional baseball on the radio. I relished the communal feasts of *carne guisada, arroz, frijoles, tortillas* and *salsa picante* that often were cooked at the brick cabin. But while others counted their cards or listened to the Astros, I roamed the brush.

Each season El Ponderosita provided us with nourishment. In the spring Papagrande and I picked *nopalitos* and yucca flowers to be sautéed with venison sausage. We cut salvia, cenizo, uña de gato, and yerba buena leaves for tea. We roasted ebony beans over hot coals and ate them like peanuts. And on several occasions, we made mesquite flour from ripe mesquite beans.

On sultry, late spring afternoons, as we sliced the immature spines and tiny leaves off nopalito pads with small pocket knives, we often talked about the brush. *"Hoy en la madrugada estaban unos coyotes ladrando tan bonito,"* Papagrande said one afternoon following an abrupt April shower. *"Yo estaba aquî tomando una taza de cafe, oyendolos. Todo era tan silencio. Los perros comensaron aya, al norte, en el otro lado de la cerca. Y luego, algunos otros comensaron al oeste. Que musica tan preciosa . . ."*

And so the conversation went: Papagrande telling me about two groups of coyotes he'd heard at daybreak. He said one pack had begun yodeling and barking somewhere to the north, then another group had answered to the west. As he spoke, my grandfather continued slicing off the nopalito spines with the precision of a surgeon. He paused and listened to the soft cooing of mourning doves, as if allowing the calm to effuse gently past us. He looked up and smiled, his pale skin furrowing under the mantle of thick bifocals.

Often we'd take the nopalitos and yucca flowers to Lita, my grandmother. She would slice the cactus into thin sections and then mix them with *chorizo con huevos,* sausage and eggs. She'd sauté the yucca flowers in a special flour mix and then serve them on the side.

In summer, we would pick the fruit from the pitaya cactus. The inch-round, bluish-bronze morsels grow on the ends of the pitaya's long, cylindrical stems. They are quite sweet. When ripe and ready to eat, the dried spines can be brushed off the fruit easily. Peel the skin from the fruit, then plump the morsel into your mouth. Not many words, all talk in whispers.

On one excursion we encountered a rattlesnake that had climbed a shrub. Always on the lookout for rattlers, but never expecting to see one three feet off the ground, we recoiled with that instinctive jerk reflex so familiar to all who live in rattlesnake country. Papagrande leveled his old Winchester model 1903 .22 auto on the snake, then said he'd never seen *un cascabel* in a bush. And I've never seen one off the ground since.

Autumn was the time of the hunt, just as it was at El Cuervo and is in all other places where men and women seek harmony with nature. I had begun hunting in Mexico and had even killed a doe, but at El Ponderosita I shot my first buck.

Uncle Trini Valverde, Jr. had taken it upon himself to teach me how to hunt deer. For the first two years I was not allowed to carry a gun. I was already a good shot by age ten, but a deer was not a rabbit or a crow. A deer demands special respect. A white-tailed deer buck is lord of the Brushlands. With his sleek, gray winter coat, his sinewy muscles, his antlers held high, his splayed nostrils breathing a steamy pulse, he is regal. A mature buck can bring out the adrenaline in a grown man with the ease of a mockingbird yanking an earthworm from moist soil.

It should be said that we did *not* hunt from a blind; that was for city folks. I learned to stalk, to walk noiselessly, to read signs. Moving with the stealth of a bobcat, sniffing the air like a coyote, eyes searching through the brush like a hawk—or sitting on trails, like stumps suddenly sprouted in the landscape, we *hunted.* Crisp morning air, chromatic golden shades of sunlight peeking through leafless mesquites, spiderwebs laced with a thousand sparkling watery diamonds, the levitating damp smell of organic earth, a hushed stillness—we *hunted.*

Suddenly a mockingbird calls, then another, and another: the Brushland telegraph sending its fleeting message that something is on the move. The camouflage-clad stump lies rigid, a gloved finger nudges a cold safety, eyes narrow, ears strain, lips dry into wrinkled paper, a cadence of heart and lungs unconsciously quickens.

By 1966 I was still nothing more than a veteran tree stump. I had shot a doe in Mexico, but does do not count. *A tree stump with no roots.* But Uncle Trini had taught me well, and he was now less of a hunter than I was becoming. In mid-December of that year, I sat on a long sendero looking east at a rising sun and at steepled thunderheads over the far-off Gulf of Mexico. Wrapped in a dark olive wool coat, a .270 at my side, I watched the doe and yearling crossing one hundred yards in front of me. I had seen them before. I had watched them nibble succulent leaves. I had listened to their subdued bleats. I had smelled the delicious odor of their bodies.

Sit still, relax, I told myself. And instantly, he appeared. Hooves bounding, neck swollen, antlers held at a rakish tilt. Time stood motionless. The rifle was at my shoulder, the crosshairs on his. I smelled the pungent stab of burnt gunpowder. I saw a white tail flicker. I stood, watching in disbelief, as if outside myself. Ten antler points lying in perfect stillness. An uncommon quiet. All life, plant and animal alike, held its breath—as it does whenever prey falls victim to predator.

Papagrande arrived at my house within minutes of my phone call, the first thing I did when I got home. He patted me on the shoulder and looked on with extreme pride. Neither he nor my uncles, his sons, had ever shot—or would ever shoot—a buck of that size.

Together we skinned the animal, then sectioned the meat for the freezer. We made plans to go back to El Ponderosita that afternoon. As we sat that evening along another sendero, watching a line of black clouds usher in a cold, blue norther, Papagrande turned, and through a wide grin, said: "Nice shot, *hijito.*" It made me feel good to know he was still thinking about my buck.

Varmint Calling

In school I met a fellow who seemed to love the woods as I did. His name was Mario Hernandez. My height, but skinnier; what he gave up in weight he made up in feistiness. I remember first seeing Mario in ninth grade history class, when he and another student were in the midst of a heated argument over who would sit at the first desk in the middle row. Mario—eyes fixed and jaw jutting out like a lizard about to fling its tongue at a fly—was not faring well. He had probably spent enough time in detention hall to know better, so he reluctantly took another chair.

This same Mario fellow was also in band with me, he on the clarinet, I on the tenor sax. When we stood next to each other in our marching formation, we'd talk about the woods. It was only natural that we become buddies.

Mario owned a Winchester model 43 in .218 Bee. At the time, all I had was a Winchester model 12, twelve gauge. But with those guns, a jar of peanut butter, a loaf of bread, and a couple of water-filled canteens, we set out to explore the wilds.

Our heroes were Jack O'Connor, Warren Page, John Hunter, Elmer Keith, and John Kingsley-Heath—all of them writers and hunters who spent their lives in Africa and Alaska, and who owned custom-made .270s, .30-06s, .375 H&H Magnums, .416 Rigbys, and .470 Nitro Expresses. I'd tell Mario that someday I'd be just like them. "Me too," Mario would say. Of course, we never guessed how much things would change.

I'm not sure whose idea it was, but I think it was mine. I had read an article on predator calling written by two brothers from Marble Falls, Texas, named Winston and Murry Burnham. The Burnham brothers had developed a small call that mimicked the cries of a dying jackrabbit. With their "varmint" call they coaxed coyotes, foxes, bobcats and other small carnivores in close enough that on occasion the critters literally jumped across their laps. Now I had seen a few coyotes: a disappearing tail as I rounded a bend in a cow path, a fuzzy blur darting across a sendero, or a loping dot working the distant end of a grassy field. Usually, the nearest I got to *el coyote* was when I heard hollow yelps and yodels on moonlit nights. The idea of being able to cajole one in close seemed too good to be true.

When the Burnham Brothers Varmint Call arrived in the mail, I opened it like a jeweler about to unwrap the Hope Diamond. The unveiling was followed by about thirty minutes of mimicking the forty-five rpm instructional record that accompanied the call. I was thankful for an understanding mother who put up with the noise. Mom had long had a strong suspicion that her son was going to be a nature lover. She tells the story of the morning when she heard the sharp, clicking noises of a great-tailed grackle coming from my upstairs bedroom. I was six months old at the time. She ran upstairs and found me standing in my crib, looking out of the window at the grackles perched in the giant tepeguaje trees that cast wide shade over our yard and onto Perkins Street. She claims I was in deep conversation with the birds, mimicking the grackles' calls perfectly. Years later, when I was about to become a teenager, Mom would take me to El Ponderosita before daybreak so that I could stand at the far southwest corner of the property and watch the sun stretch pink tentacles through the brush. When I'd walk back to the car she'd always ask what I had seen. Then she would listen intently as I went through long descriptions of bird and animal sightings.

I practiced with the Burnham Brothers call until I sounded just like the jackrabbit on the forty-five rpm record. But it was another few weeks before I actually called a coyote. On that fateful day, Mario and I were perched on a rocky ledge overlooking the remnants of an old gravel pit. A thick layer of misting clouds had reduced visibility to less than a hundred yards. Cold and wet we crouched, wrapped in army surplus jackets and with felt hats yanked awkwardly over our ears. I cradled my father's 12 gauge, Mario his .218 Bee. We were beginning to think that this calling business was a hoax. I lifted the frigid call to my mouth, took a deep breath, and proceeded to blow a series of lamenting cries into the dark afternoon sky. Nothing happened. Just as on the five or six excursions that had preceded this one. No throng of coyotes came rushing out of the brush beelining it to the dying jackrabbit that wasn't there. No bobcat scurried up a tree to check out the area. No gray fox scampered over the ridge. Instead, all remained still. I glanced at Mario; he raised his eyebrows. I lifted the call to my chapped lips and blew more shrills into the fog. *Nothing* . . .

The procedure was repeated another three or four times. Thirty slow-motion minutes had elapsed. The mist had turned into a drizzle. I was about to give it one last try when Mario nudged me. His eyes were darting toward the back, his eyebrows simultaneously crunched in the same direction. Either he was having a fit, or something was behind us. I turned slowly. *Yes!* A dark creature—head held low, wet fur ruffled—stalked to within a few feet. Then it began to circle, nose held out as it sniffed the wind. But this was happening too quickly. If we moved, we'd be spotted. The beast, which I was pretty darn sure would prove to be a coyote, would be gone in an instant. So we sat, like two paralyzed rabbits, soaked and shivering. The animal ventured closer—*it was a coyote all right*—looked us over, then, as mysteriously as it had appeared, it vanished, lost behind a stand of purple sage.

For nearly a minute, neither Mario nor I spoke. Finally, we stood, brushed the cold, wet dirt off our pants, stretched our legs and backs, and offered quiet cheers.

At least we'd learned that calling from the ground was no good. Coyotes, bobcats, and other predators can spot the slightest movement at ground level. They spend their lives searching the landscape for prey. If we cried out like a rabbit, then they would be especially tuned. To be successful we would have to climb trees. We also knew that we needed to expand our territory. Once an area has been "called" it takes a long time to get results again, because coyotes will not return to be tricked a second time. Fences and No Trespassing signs might have been a hindrance, but we conveniently concluded that life was too short to pay attention to laws that forbade people to see the land.

One day we parked my Volkswagen at the end of a dirt road, hustled out, and ducked under the fence. A minute later we were surrounded by big mesquite and ebony trees. Our routine was to examine each mesquite, searching for one that was the right size, with thick trunks and branches high enough to offer a good perch and suitable concealment. Finding the correct tree, we would silently assaulted it like commandos scaling a cliff. Once we reached the lookout point, we evolved into wingless birds scanning the countryside.

The day was cloudless, with a cool breeze brushing our faces like fine silk. Mario had decided to climb a tree about fifty yards away from mine, so I waited for him to settle down, then blew a series of tortured notes. In the distance, I could see a caracara flying toward us. This was a common sight. Hawks and owls came frequently to the call. I blew again, and waited some more. Suddenly, the brush exploded with gleeful yelps and hoots. Barks and yodels, like waves traversing a pool, swooshed from one end of the woods to the other. The racket reached a maniacal zenith, then waned into silence.

Mario's .218 Bee cracked the instant the barking stopped. And like magic, coyotes appeared from everywhere. Five ran directly under my tree. Several others hightailed it past a cow trail not twenty feet from my stand. Then, as quickly as it had begun, the action was over. I waited another minute before retracing my ascent route back to ground level. When I came to Mario's tree it was abandoned. Then I heard a whistle. To my right I saw a skinny frame, atop lanky legs, on which was propped Mario's toothy grin. At his feet lay a handsome coyote. I don't know which of us was more thrilled. We shook hands and danced a jig. We were now varmint callers.

Mario and I constantly tried to outdo each other. Who was the better tracker, sign cutter, stalker, hunter, the best shot? But at the same time, we enjoyed the fact that neither surpassed the other. In our minds we, together, were the best.

As our woodsmanship skills developed, so did our arrogance. One day while hunting a few miles east of El Ponderosita, we spotted a group of hunter—trespassers like us. We boldly approached them and said: "What are you guys doing on this land?" Of course, they had no idea we weren't the land owners, so they humbly apologized and beat a quick retreat. We went about our business, which was mainly exploring, climbing trees, pretending to be dying rabbits, and identifying birds and plants.

A sure cure for arrogance was the *pamorana* ant, for which we were always on the lookout when we climbed mesquites. Pamoranas are about half an inch long. Their brindled black and gray coloring makes them nearly impossible to spot on the black and gray trunks of mesquite trees. Pamoranas are extremely aggressive and bite fiercely. The sight of just one big ant crawling on a trunk or limb was enough to warrant hasty abandonment. We learned this precaution the hard way.

By the summer of 1966 Mario and I had taken to spending days at El Ponderosita. We'd pack food, enough water for a week, sleeping bags, and two canvas cots. Early mornings and evenings were spent exploring. The hot midday was for reading, watching the clouds, and listening to the droning chant of cicadas intermixed with the hypnotic coos of mourning doves. At night we'd sleep on the roof of the cabin's porch.

About one hundred yards past the west fence line was a particularly fine mesquite tree. One morning, we decided to call from that tree. I grabbed one of the stout lower limbs, chinned myself up and proceeded to reach the highest branches, some thirty feet above the ground. Mario selected a barrel-thick branch about ten feet below me. The day was perfect for calling. There was no wind, which meant that the screeches of the varmint call would carry farther in the stillness.

I checked the call to make sure no bits of bark had fallen into it, then proceeded to announce our presence. From my stand, I could see a hundred feet in all directions. Now it was time to sit still and see what would happen. Instead, I heard, *"Ants!"*

Mario was slapping his pants—mumbling and cursing and trying to keep his rifle from falling to the ground while he hurried off the tree. Then I spotted them: legions of angry pamoranas marching upward, a military sortie with one objective—annihilate the green-eyed fool in jeans and T-shirt. There was nothing to do, no way to crawl back down. It was jump or be eaten alive.

Mario said later that all he could hear was the snapping of branches as I plummeted earthward. I hit the soft dirt, then pogo-sticked skyward, all the while checking myself for ants. Fortunately, I was unscathed. Mario, however, was into phase two of post-pamorana shock. He turned pale and threw up.

Back at camp—Mario still dizzy and nauseous—we contemplated the sanity of climbing ant-infested trees. He swore he'd never call from a mesquite again. "Sound wisdom," I returned.

As the months passed, we spent less time varmint calling and more time brush roaming. Often, I would take one trail, Mario another. It was the way that, in due course, we would both go. After high school we took different paths.

In the evenings, following an afternoon of wandering the brush, we'd describe the things we had seen—a woodsman's way of counting coup. Embellishment was considered an adjunct to good story telling. And Mario was a card-carrying expert at stretching the truth. Naturally, I tried my best to emulate him, though he always claimed I was a pathetic neophyte.

Our woods skills grew. Mario called me the Blood Hound because I could smell deer, badgers, javelina, and other critters long before we encountered them. I called him *Indio* because he loved to track. I can still see him stooping beside a spiny crucifixion thorn or pausing on a cow trail. "This," he'd say, "is a skunk track (or deer track, or javelina track) and it's *exactly* three (or four, or five) days old."

In the end, after many adventures in the woods, the last thing we wanted was to spoil the Brushland quiet with a rifle shot. We became obsessed with silence. But remaining silent was a problem when we encountered rattlesnakes.

Sometimes there seemed to be as many rattlesnakes as pamoranas. Whoever walked in the lead kept his eyes on the ground. The man in back looked ahead to negotiate the trail and spot animals. At least, that was the plan.

On days when there were too many rattlers, we'd acquire a sort of shell shock. We'd retreat, disgusted and depressed, back to the car or to the brick cabin at El Ponderosita. There was no way to get around some rattlesnakes, especially if we were in heavy brush, and so they had to be killed. If we could, we'd use a long stick to dispatch them. Other times, there was no choice but to fire a round.

Looking back, our experiences were entirely positive. Had we not given ourselves such constant exposure to the brush, it is unlikely that we would have grown into the nature lovers we both are today. But, of course, all things change; it is a revelation that strikes some harder than others. After high school, Mario and I went our separate ways. He was too impetuous and high strung to finish college. Perhaps I would have floundered as well had my parents not been so obstinate about higher education.

Strange thing, though, that formal schooling did not offer either of us the foundation that was to carry us through the later years. That gift came from our experiences in the Brushlands.

Rattlesnakes

If asked to choose which animal rules the Brushlands, I would unhesitatingly pick the western diamondback rattlesnake. No other beast is as fierce, unrelenting, and downright dangerous as the rattler. Other Brushland creatures are majestic or beautiful, but none combine beauty, majesty, and ferocity the way the diamondback does. A six-foot rattler poised to strike—it's ominous, triangular head rooted atop the graceful arch of its body; its sinister tongue darting like a laser guidance system homing in on target; and the distinctive buzz from rattles vibrating too fast for the eye to track—makes a picture that the mind does not soon forget. The western diamondback fears nothing, and it rarely goes on the defensive. Once committed it will fight to the death—of its prey or of itself.

I was thirteen when I shot my first rattlesnake. It was during a family visit to El Cuervo ranch in Mexico. Doña Paz, foreman Don Teodoro's wife, had invited my mother, sister, and me to see a cave near the San Fernando River. The region was not known for caves, which made this strange hole in the ground that much more of a curiosity. Legend had it that a band of outlaws had dug the cave back in the late 1800s. As the story went, *los bandidos* had robbed a bank in Ciudad Victoria and were being chased by Mexican lawmen and soldiers. In order to obscure their trail, the outlaws built a small raft east of the town of San Fernando, with plans to float down the San Fernando River until they reached the coast. From there they hoped to sail north to Texas.

Making a run for the border was not a one-way affair at the time.

Just as outlaws from Texas regularly sought refuge in Mexico, Mexican bandits headed north for Texas, New Mexico, Arizona, or California. Even today Mexican fugitives flee to the United States; the Rio Grande Valley remains a popular hideout. For some reason the plan in this case went awry and los bandidos were forced to abandon their raft after traveling only twenty miles. They dismantled the boat and let the pieces float down the river, like so much debris washing into the Gulf of Mexico.

The bandits then spent nearly a month hollowing out a tunnel in which to hide, or to cache their loot in the event the soldiers and lawmen got too close. As luck would have it, the bandits dug their way into a small, natural cavern, which was protected overhead by a huge limestone slab.

When we visited the old hideout we found a four-foot-wide gaping hole. The sunlight showed that it plunged into the earth for about ten feet before angling off. Doña Paz said the tunnel paralleled the surface for another ten feet then opened into a chamber approximately twenty feet square. She added that the underground room had once held the remnants of a saddle and some rusting pots and pans. But by 1962 those artifacts were long gone, as were most of the mesquite beams that had been used to support the clay soil overlying the tunnel.

As we peered into the foreboding hole, we noticed a slithering object approaching from the right. The snake was only about four feet long, but it was determined. It came directly at us. All in one swift move, Mom, sis, and Doña Paz reconvened their conversation within the car, while I tried desperately to untangle the .22 rifle from the legs and skirts that had somehow shoved it onto the floorboard. At last, I was able to get the gun out and pointed in the direction of the snake, now only a few feet away.

The sole advice I'd ever heard about rattlers had been to shoot for the head—nothing else would do. I heeded that warning, and a volley of bullets from the little Stevens auto quickly disintegrated the snake's anterior end.

Afterward, Mom, sis, and Doña Paz gathered around the immobile and headless creature. They gawked and exchanged opinions. It was then that Doña Paz remembered her husband and others commenting on how the cave was the gathering place for diamondbacks during the late fall and winter.

But I recall that it was late summer when the incident occurred. And of the thousands of rattlesnakes I have encountered since then, I have *never*—except for that first time—been "charged" by a single one. There is no other way to describe it. The snake came at us like a runaway train.

"What good is a rattlesnake?" In Texas that attitude has been unrelenting. When I was a boy, deep South Texas seemed infested with diamondbacks. They had plenty of food. The brush was teeming with kangaroo rats and mice; woodrat nests choked almost every clump of prickly pear cactus. There were also hordes of pygmy mice, grasshopper mice, and white-footed mice. Abundant prey allowed for ample predators.

The diamondback suffers from one great handicap, however. Despite its lightning-fast strike, it is a lethargic reptile. In fact, when compared to an indigo or corn snake, the rattlesnake appears stuck in perpetual slow motion. To overcome its sluggish pace, the rattlesnake must rely on stealth; its camouflaged skin and its ability to move noiselessly enable it to sneak up on prey. When the brush began to disappear, however, the great diamondback could no longer compete. An indigo snake, for example, can rush through grass and overtake its prey. Western diamondbacks, on the other hand, are at a distinct disadvantage when away from thick brush, because mice and other rodents can readily outrun them.

But back in the 1950s and 1960s there seemed no threat to the upland brush or to the great western diamondback rattlesnakes that lived within it. And if we were lectured incessantly about watching out for snakes, it was because the likelihood of seeing one was considerable.

My mother's family knew well the terror that rattlesnakes wrought. In 1937, as a boy, my Uncle Trini Valverde was bitten by a small rattlesnake as he lay sleeping in the family home in northern Starr County. Ironically, Uncle Trini's older brother, Bill, had just returned from a stay in Rio Grande City, where he had been treated for burns received while trying to flush a large rattlesnake from its den. Uncle Bill had poured gasoline down one opening of the den and then put a match to it. Not far away was another hole. Uncle Bill did not know that the two holes were connected, and when he poured gasoline into the second hole he was instantly engulfed in flames.

Usually, Uncle Trini and Uncle Bill slept together on a double bed in one of the house's three small bedrooms. But because Uncle Bill was convalescing from his burns, he was in bed that night with my grandmother, Lita. Sometime before midnight, Uncle Trini started complaining that his finger hurt.

"Mama, Mama," he moaned, *"me duele un dedo."*

Thinking little Trini merely wanted some attention, Lita checked his finger; she found it slightly swollen.

"It's probably just a thorn," she said. "We'll take care of it tomorrow morning."

Several hours passed, but the pain only grew worse. *"Mama, por favor—duele mi dedo!"*

Sometime after midnight, my tired grandmother rose one more time to check on little Trini. But this time there was instant alarm. His finger had swollen to the point where it seemed it might burst. It was then that my grandmother removed the sheet and spotted the rattlesnake coiled next to her nine-year-old.

Lita called my grandfather into the room. Trini had been complaining for several hours. Both my grandparents realized that their small son would die if he didn't receive immediate treatment.

While my mother, Ella, fueled the family car at my grandfather's service station next door, my grandparents placed an urgent call to the family doctor, Cayetano Barrera, in Mission. Dr. Barrera was related to my grandmother and was a close family friend. He told them he would meet them on the narrow dirt road that connected the Starr County hamlet of San Isidro with the town of Mission, some thirty miles away in Hidalgo County. He added that he would bring antivenin.

Dawn was approaching when the drivers finally glimpsed each other's headlights. Fortunately, there had been no storms, because the road would have been impassible had it been drenched by recent rains. In the anxiety of the moment, however, Dr. Barrera had forgotten the antivenin back at his clinic in Mission. There was no time to waste. The doctor had the faster car, so he instructed my grandparents to switch the child into his auto, and together they disappeared into the twilight. One can only imagine what was going through my grandmother's mind as she watched her young son being driven away.

Uncle Trini lived. But having learned the hard way, the Valverde family never forgot how dangerous rattlesnakes can be. Each time I ventured into the brush as a boy, I was told, *"mucho quidado con las viboras."*

In the ensuing years, I've learned the following lessons about rattlesnakes. *Lesson Number One:* Rattlesnakes don't always rattle before they bite. *Lesson Number Two:* Never freeze (like in the movies) when you come upon a rattler. *Lesson Number Three:* Dead rattlesnakes can still bite you. *Lesson Number Four:* Small rattlesnakes can deliver more lethal blows than large rattlesnakes. *Lesson Number Five:* Rattlesnakes sometimes come in pairs. *Lesson Number Six:* Within the first twenty-four hours after a rattlesnake bite, more people die from shock than from the effects of the snake's venom. *Lesson Number Seven:* Rattlesnakes are most active at night. *Lesson Number Eight:* Most rattlesnakes strike below the knee, but big snakes can hit as high as the groin. *Lesson Number Nine:* Lancing a bite can hasten the effects of the venom. *Lesson Number Ten:* The danger zone around a coiled rattler is about half the distance of the snake's body.

Someone who has never had a close encounter with a rattlesnake, or who has grown up in a place that allows no genuine experiences among diamondbacks, may disagree with the old dictum that the only good rattlesnake is a dead rattlesnake.

Of course, that cliché falls short of the truth. But in the old days, the poignant Brushland ethos had it that a rattler unexorcised of life was a devil free to haunt elsewhere. Besides, living and letting live made sense only when both sides agreed. We therefore killed rattlesnakes by the hundreds.

They were not always easy to "kill." Stories about rattlers biting even after they were dead abound. Back in the early 1960's a particularly tantalizing tale to that effect circulated through the deer camps of northern Starr County.

It seems a group of Houston "hunters" had leased a ranch near the town of La Gloria. They had towed several travel trailers to their lease, planning to mix hunting with other pleasures. During the Thanksgiving holidays the fellows had arranged a rendezvous with some "ladies" who had also driven down from the big city.

When the coterie arrived at the ranch gate, they observed a large rattlesnake coiled near the padlock. "Don't worry," said one of the hunters, who extracted his pistol from his glove compartment and fired a bullet into the snake's head. The serpent went limp; it was surely dead. The man picked up the snake and proclaimed to his companions that it was going to make a dandy hatband once skinned and dried. He then threw the snake onto the floorboard of his car, despite his lady friend's protests.

On the bumpy road to camp the lady suddenly jerked her leg up, writhing in pain. "What now?" asked her companion. She wailed that the snake had bitten her. "Can't be," said the man. "I shot it in the head—it's dead."

By the time they reached the camp, the woman was in agony. Their friends, who had driven up in their own vehicles, gathered around. The man reached down to pick the dead snake off the floorboard and was promptly bitten on the wrist. They were rushed to a hospital in McAllen (others say Laredo) where they were treated. The woman lost most of the muscle tissue beneath the knee and above the ankle. The man lost three fingers from his right hand. But the interesting part (as the story goes) was that the wife of One-Shot-in-the-Head came from a wealthy Houston family. His money was actually her money, and when she realized what had been going on, he was rapidly separated from it.

So how do dead snakes bite? Basically it has to do with the flow of ions across cell membranes and the availability of energy-containing ATP (Adenosine triphosphate), which leads to muscle contractions. Biologists call the phenomena "action potentials" and "muscle filament sliding."

Action potentials create the ionic polar reversals that lead to muscle tissue contraction. For a very short time after death, muscle contractions continue as electrochemical gradients change across the muscle cell's membrane, and remaining ATP binds to the thick-filament muscle fibers on tiny hammerlike attachments that, given ATP's energy, yank the thin filaments past them. But since cellular respiration (the mechanism that transfers energy along metabolic pathways) no longer occurs after death, the hammerlike attachments found on the thick filaments of each muscle cell run out of ATP, and so they eventually become firmly attached to the thin filaments; this is what causes rigor mortis. In the interim, the transient combination of action potentials across cell membranes and the remaining ATP enables a dead snake to continue moving and to "bite," though this is a completely involuntary action. To be safe, therefore, a rattlesnake's head should be removed from its body before anyone handles the carcass.

Once snake bitten, the only safe procedure is to seek medical attention immediately.

A case of what *not* to do after a snake bite comes from the early days of bow hunting at Laguna Atascosa National Wildlife Refuge. Laguna Atascosa, which means "muddy lagoon," is famous for its rattlesnakes. Located in northeastern Cameron County, between the shores of the salty Laguna Madre and the brackish Laguna Atascosa, the refuge harbors an immense array of seasonal waterfowl and land birds, as well as goodly populations of white-tailed deer, javelina, coyotes, bobcats, ocelots, feral pigs, alligators, *and* western diamondback rattlesnakes.

The bow hunter who arrived at the refuge checkout station was pale and barely able to walk. In a panicked voice, he said, "I've been snake bit. I used my knife to cut the poison out." The man's speech was beginning to slur, his eyes were rolling back. In another hour he would have died, though not from the snake's bite but from loss of blood.

Perhaps he had watched too many westerns and believed that lancing a pit viper's bite was the correct thing to do. Had he known better, he would have left the wound alone—aware that the human body deploys its own defenses within seconds after a bite. According to the medical doctors I've spoken to, the body creates a sort of capsule (assuming no major blood vessel has been punctured) that surrounds the venom and keeps it, for as much as twelve hours, from traversing into adjacent tissues. If the bite is cut open, the capsule is destroyed and the body's initial defense against the venom is rendered useless.

If you are bitten by a rattlesnake, try—(I admit it won't be easy, but *try*) to walk back to your car, then seek the nearest professional medical help. As in the case of my Uncle Trini, as long as the body's own protective capsule is not broken, the chances for complete recovery are good, and the possibility of having to lose a limb is lessened. Be warned, however, that small rattlesnakes often inflict more lethal doses of venom than do larger snakes. The big snakes seem able to control the amount of venom they inject. Two- and three-foot snakes, on the other hand, go for broke. They deliver nearly all their venom on the first blow.

As to what to do when one encounters a rattlesnake in the brush, that depends on the exact situation. Needless to say, vigilance supersedes all other advice. Long-time brush roamers may look as if they are lost in thought or carried away by the beauty surrounding them. But I assure you that they have one eye, and a great deal of their mental acuity, fixed on the possibility that yonder clump of grass might harbor a coiled tribulation.

And if you stumble onto a rattlesnake, do not freeze, as is often advised. Get the hell out of striking distance, *pronto.* If you freeze and then move slowly, you are most likely going to get bitten. Rattlesnakes key on the freezing behaviors of rabbits, rats, and mice. They will therefore strike if your leg starts behaving like a rabbit, rat, or mouse. But if you leap out of the way the snake will be confused, and even if it does strike, it will probably miss.

During the mating season, rattlesnakes often bunch into mating groups. If you walk into an orgy of amorous diamondbacks, then you should tiptoe out, since the snakes at that moment do not have rabbits, rats, and mice on their minds.

A good pair of snake leggings, a comfortable pair of leather boots, and especially a goodly portion of common sense go a long ways toward preventing a French kiss from *un vibora cascabel.*

In deep South Texas—before the days of computer games and MTV; before drugs and gangs; before "men and women of vision" destroyed the land—young couples took leisurely drives hunting for rattlesnakes along the county roads that cut through the Brushlands. My next-door neighbor, Anne Blankenbaker, and I would spend hours on summer evenings creeping along the isolated roads of western Hidalgo and eastern Starr counties. I behind the steering wheel, Anne riding shotgun, we'd search for the ancient monarch, its heavy body coursing sinuous waves through the sand as it crossed from one side of the road to the other.

We carelessly talked of the future, never realizing that the past would someday be the object of much more intense conversation. But traveling within the tempered quiet of a slow-moving car—juxtaposed by a claret-red sun riding the present into eternity—how could either of us have known that what we had at that moment was unique?

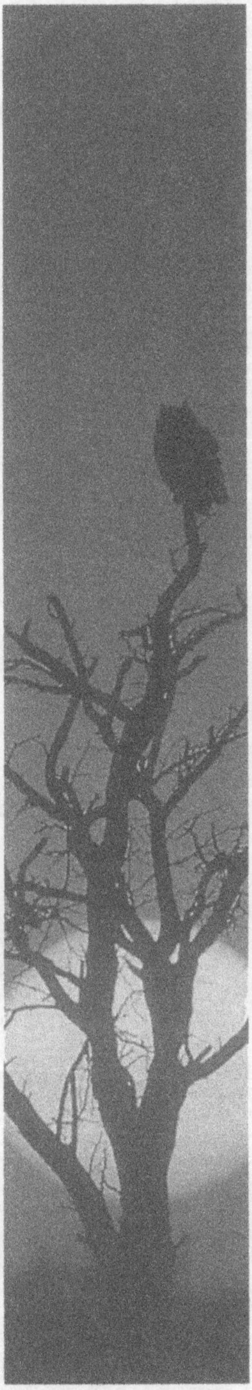

Part II
The Dark Years

Bulldozers and Rootplows

South Texas serves as a good example of how a strong politically conservative block—a group quick to lambaste the welfare state and socialism—is itself wedded to government handouts and manipulating "the system." In the Rio Grande Valley, the word *conservative,* as is common throughout this country, often has less to do with conservation than it has to do with politically acceptable exploitation based on greed. In fact, it is ironic that those who are most to blame for the devastation of habitat—whether by indiscriminate bulldozing and rootplowing or by the unbridled dumping of pesticides and defoliants—are themselves lauded (by their own) as men and women of vision and as leaders of the community.[1]

That this paradox has been allowed to persist (where destruction is viewed as something good) speaks directly to the ethic, or lack thereof, that has existed toward the land. But in order to understand how something so plainly contradictory could become acceptable and commonplace, one must first examine the history of the area and the mindset of those who settled it.

The history of deforestation in deep South Texas begins shortly before the end of the nineteenth century when the second great wave of Anglo immigrants began to arrive.[2] Preceding the influx of these Anglo farmers, deep South Texas—roughly that area south of a line drawn west from Corpus Christi to Laredo, encompassing all the land within the northern confines of the Rio Grande—was made up of a mosaic of lush mesquite chaparral and grassy savanna.

Some biologists have argued that deep South Texas was entirely a grassland, with small motts of chaparral. The prevailing theory submits that the deliberate halting of grass fires prompted an expansion of the brush. However, in the lower Rio Grande Valley—Starr, Hidalgo, Cameron, and Willacy counties—evidence suggests that dense mesquite *monte* was always the prevailing ecotype. In his excellent treatise entitled *Indians of the Rio Grande Delta,* anthropologist Martin Salinas presents descriptions of the region based on the writings of the first Spanish explorers who traversed it.[3] Salinas notes that "only by documentary research and the study of small relict areas is it possible to gain impressions of what the delta area as a whole was really like when inhabited only by American Indians."[4] According to Salinas, Spanish explorers wrote that the land we now call the Rio Grande Valley (especially the expanse running south to the river from a line drawn west through the towns of Raymondville, Edcouch, Edinburg, Mission, and La Joya) underwent periods of intense flooding. Lakes and swamps were mingled profusely between weaving riparian tracts, creating a landscape that in many places resembled jungle rather than desert scrub. Salinas suggests that the first inhabitants of the delta traversed this biotically rich mosaic of *resacas* (ox-bow lakes), ponds, and meandering tributaries via those lush serpentine woods. Farther north, however, according to Salinas, the Spaniards found a large area essentially devoid of human life. This sandy, dry region includes a large part of Jim Hogg, Brooks, and Kenedy counties.

Nonetheless, the early Spanish explorers found the Rio Grande Valley (including western Starr County and on into Zapata and Webb counties) an almost impenetrable forest of mesquite and ebony mingled with dense thorny thickets. In 1686, the Spanish explorer Alonso de Léon observed that Indians had been forced to hack trails through the monte near the present town of Reynosa, Tamaulipas, in order to travel from one camp to another.[5] These trails, called *brechas* by the Spanish, proved to be the common means by which Indians from different bands communicated with one another. One such brecha proved to be a life saver for a Spanish surveying party in 1777 when they became hopelessly lost in impenetrable brush near the border of Hidalgo and Cameron counties. Salinas writes that a group of Pauraque Indians found the Spaniards and escorted them out of the brush by way of a trail.

The dense delta monte was not without a few barren patches. Indians used these small openings as campsites, but the brush was their source for food (both animal and plant), building materials, medicines, weapons, and for safety. In 1772, a Spanish expedition noted that a group of Mulato Indians had placed their camp in an open area next to thick brush to ensure that in case of attack, they could disappear in a flash.[6]

Folk tales from families whose ancestors settled South Texas as far back as the late 1700s also describe the Rio Grande Valley as a land of intensely thick brush. The Benito Treviño family from Starr County, for example, tells the story of a great, great uncle named Pablo Treviño who worked as a wagon master in the mid- to late 1800s. Pablo Treviño traveled often from the ranches in Starr County to the port of Brownsville to pick up supplies. He could never travel a straight route, however, because the delta was either choked with brush or under water. Instead, his route to Brownsville was always a circuitous trek to the north then east, through the sandy savannas that today make up parts of Jim Hogg, Brooks, and Kenedy counties.

Former Texas DPS narcotics agent Joe Garza from McAllen is a direct descendant of Manuel Vela, who operated a way station in southern Jim Hogg County for wagons coming out of the ranches of what are now Starr, Zapata, and Webb counties. From Vela's Station, the wagons followed routes to the ports of Brownsville and Corpus Christi.

The Garza family's ranch El Puerto in Jim Hogg County harbors the original way station built by Manuel Vela's father in the mid-1800s. In 1879 the compound was attacked by Indians, and the roof was burned beyond repair. Manuel ordered that a new roof be constructed; the original building and this roof, with "1879" written on the ceiling, have been carefully preserved. Until the late 1970s, the old wagon trails, cutting through miles of a diverse spectrum of Brushland plants, could still be seen. The descendants of Manuel Vela cherish the folk tales of bandit attacks and Indian raids that took place at or near Rancho El Puerto. The legends always underscore the fact that the land was heavy brush, with monte sprawling to the south and west as far as the eye could see.

From the eastern Rio Grande Valley come folk tales of adventurers who smuggled weapons into Mexico in the late 1800s and early 1900s via hidden trails through the junglelike woods of Cameron and Willacy counties, and who during Prohibition, using similar trails, smuggled alcohol into the United States—although even by that time, concerted efforts by farmers had begun to destroy the woodlands of those counties.[7] One such character was Casimiro Garcia. His real name was Francisco, but when he became a wanted man in Mexico during the Mexican Revolution, he adopted his late brother's name in order to foil the law. Throughout Prohibition, Casimiro made a living by keeping a number of bordellos and beer joints in South Texas stocked with booze. He was never caught. He used to tell friends before his death in 1975 that *el monte obscuro* (the dark woods) protected him from *los Rinches*—the Texas Rangers. Atop a stalky pony, his .44-40 Winchester carbine cradled in a worn scabbard and with two or three mules laden with tequila and rum straddling behind, Casimiro rode in the dark silence of moonless nights—his nose trained to catch the faintest smell of a lit cigarette or a distant mesquite campfire; his ears tuned to the subtle messages of croaking frogs gone suddenly silent. He knew that no one had gone before him as long as spiderwebs continued to brush his face.

But the great blanket of woods that greeted the first Spanish explorers, and had been home for countless generations of Indians, soon disappeared when the Midwestern farmers arrived. With the frenzy of termites they denuded the land of its bountiful forests. They drained ponds and lakes and then began to build canals to channel water from the Rio Grande inland. By 1935 most of the rich riparian woodlands of the delta had been wiped out. Only scattered remnants, like tiny wonderlands, remained.

The upland brush, however, stayed relatively unscathed until about the mid-1960s. This was a drier land where mesquites did not often surpass twenty feet in height. Nonetheless, as the Spanish had discovered three centuries before, it was an immense thicket extending for many miles and interrupted by only an occasional dot of grass. Unfortunately, this land was not to be spared. Cows, after all, prefer grassland.

Though range research is widening in focus today, scientific inquiry has too often been subtly biased toward promoting the introduction of grasses for cattle grazing. Proclaim that an area is "all grass," and it becomes easier and less disturbing to the conscience to rationalize bulldozing and rootplowing the monte. The two go together: generally dragged behind a bulldozer, a rootplow consists of a row of steel teeth, which literally shreds plant roots. This became the common theme after the 1960s. Range scientists—like road engineers obsessed with creating more highways—claimed that deep South Texas had been predominantly a grassland and that it should be returned to grassland conditions. They asserted that the monte had begun to increase only *after* natural fires were curtailed. Evidence suggests that in some locales farther north and in other parts of the world, habitats changed after fires were inhibited. But in the Rio Grande Valley of Texas it was not so. The delta and the upland clay soils extending north nearly to the towns of Encino and Hebbronville were covered with brush. Only amidst the eolian sands *beyond* those towns was there savanna.

In fact, it has been suggested that grassland was the unnatural situation in deep South Texas, since monte persists much longer—especially if it consists of diverse woody plants, which are relatively resilient to abiotic stresses. Albeit all ecosystems are in a constant state of flux, and truly optimum equilibria remain elusive at best, nonetheless the monte—because of its tendency to resist environmental trauma—is inherently more stable than grassland and therefore represents a more mature ecosystem.

By 1960, the irrigable delta of deep South Texas was firmly in the hands of a few land barons who controlled the politics and the economy. The political lines between the farmers of the delta region and the ranchers of the upland brush, which had still to see the ravages of the bulldozer, were almost as clearly marked as the gashes made by the northernmost irrigation canals.

Throughout the 1900s the upland brush that sprawled across Starr County into northern Hidalgo County, and sent ribbons into remote sections of Willacy County, had been relegated to the ranches. The chaparral was "cattle country," and as long as it took twenty acres or more to feed one cow, the ranchers would be economically and politically subservient to the big farmers. All that changed when oil was discovered. Overnight, ranchers became "oil men." The cowboy life dissolved into a hobby, a facade at pretend work; the real income came from those huge, wingless, iron birds that pecked the ground, endlessly consuming the thick, black water that lay underneath.

But a writhing avarice followed this newfound wealth. Whether by political manipulation or just plain stupidity, the U.S. government began paying landowners to clear the brush. The federally funded land clearing programs, however, were almost immediately fraught with impropriety. Unscrupulous speculators began purchasing tracts of brush with the express purpose of bulldozing in order to make a fast buck at taxpayers' expense. With money in pocket, these speculators often abandoned the land or dumped it by selling it for nothing down, with low monthly payments and high interest rates. More often than not, the land—now void of brush cover—quickly eroded into something not far removed from desert.

But ranchers were not the only ones to glimpse that pot of gold at the end of the Washington, D.C., rainbow. Farmers, who had made great efforts to ensure that local, state, and federal politicians viewed the world from an "agricultural perspective," also cast covetous eyes on Uncle Sam's coffer. A farmer could make money by bulldozing brush, then be assured of a constant dole through subsidies and other government giveaways. As a result, the lands around McCook were turned into a moonscape by 1970. The brush between Edinburg and San Manuel was nearly all rootplowed by 1975. The territory north of Sullivan City had become windswept and desolate by 1977.

I was a young man still trying to figure out my course in life when I came face to face with the ravages of the bulldozer and rootplow. The thousand-acre brush tract north of El Ponderosita was pushed into gigantic piles and burned in less than a week in May, 1969. Traversing the land was a fifty-yard wide emerald ribbon, where trees and shrubs reached three times the height of the surrounding vegetation, marking the route of a slow moving, sub-surface stream. These riparian-like corridors which were once common in western Hidalgo County and throughout Starr County, but which have been nearly all destroyed, are called *ramaderos.* Derived from the Spanish word *ramada,* a mass of branches, these passageways, within which summer temperatures are reduced by as much as ten degrees, serve as migratory pathways for monarch butterflies, and as shelter for many Brushland birds and mammals.

I was not aware of what had happened until I rounded the sendero on the far northwest side of my uncle's ranchito. The brush was now nothing more than stubble. Mesquites with trunks measuring three feet in diameter lay broken and crumpled, as if a tornado had cut a mile-wide swath across the earth. The prickly pear cactus, purple sage, palo verde, coma, ebony, pitaya, uña de gato, salvia, huisache, and all the other plants that kept the soil in check, that gave food and shelter to the wildlife, and that attracted the rains were now heaped together like decaying bodies waiting for mass cremation. I stood speechless, full of rage.

Two days later smoke plumes rose off the land into a lifeless, black sky—the sun but a dim, orange ball beyond. At night the light from a hundred bonfires reflected against an opaque mass of smoke. "Hell hath come," I said aloud. There was no place to turn my anger, so it went inward. I began to wither, no less wounded than the earth surrounding me.

Over the next ten years the destruction continued, as if someone had unleashed the devil to pillage the earth at will. I drove down county roads that had once been bordered by lush woods. Now the roads were simply a deeper gash in a land mutilated and scarred. The destruction was relentless, as if every briary patch was nothing more than a potential grub steak waiting to be roasted in order to sate the appetites of political and economic expediency. And yet I was as helpless as the brush to act.

One afternoon in the fall of 1973 I stood atop a small hill between Rio Grande City and La Gloria and watched four bulldozers desecrating the earth. They worked relentlessly, columns of charcoal exhaust puffing from their noisy diesel engines. Into the night—floodlights illuminating their paths—they laid waste the life that had grown free for countless millennia. At last, overwhelmed by emotion, I wept in the darkness.

I spent the night on that hill. In the wee morning hours, deer fleeing for their lives ran past me. And, a group of perhaps twenty javelina wandered by looking confused and disoriented. When the first meager shades of tarnished yellow sunrise surfaced behind me, I looked on in horror at what had occurred during the night. It was as if a great monster had erased the landscape. What had been was now gone. Only blistered earth remained. *Glory hallelujah to man and his machines . . .*

The Darkness

In August, 1973, I took a quick trip to Albuquerque, New Mexico, because I wanted to be in the mountains: a place too steep and rugged for any bulldozer to make a successful foray. Besides, I just needed to get away. Papagrande, T. M. Valverde, Sr., had died the previous June. I had not been able to grieve. At the funeral I stood stoically watching my relatives mourn. But my eyes remained dry. Papagrande had died a lingering death; cancer never lets its victims go peacefully.

On the last day of his life, as he lay emaciated in his bed, he somehow managed to smile when he saw me. He had not recognized two of my cousins who had stood briefly by his side. But when his eyes met mine, he offered a trembling grin. That night, after he had breathed his last, I walked into the room and glanced at his quiet face. But I could not cry.

Though Albuquerque lay pressed against the mountains, it was just another cluster of high-rise office buildings, cramped apartments, generic shopping malls, monotonous housing tracts, congested traffic, and smog.

I was newly married, and I had a six-month-old baby boy. The marriage was not faring well, but my little boy was the most beautiful creature I had ever seen. I worried constantly for his welfare. And when the friends we were visiting suggested we eat at a vegetarian restaurant, I figured it was a good place to go. Unfortunately, like a lot of places espousing "the clean life," this was more a hippy joint than a place to take a family. As I entered the restaurant, I noticed that the rock music was horribly loud. I instantly became concerned for my baby's hearing, and at that moment a feeling of panic overwhelmed me.

I had no idea what was happening. Everything suddenly became unreal. My heart raced, so I walked back to the car where, for what seemed an eternity, I labored within the vising grip of fear. My heart skipped beats and then sped even faster. All the while things became more unreal; I was looking at the world as if it was a distant movie. The more I tried to make contact with my surroundings, the more disassociated the picture became.

Later that afternoon I was taken to a hospital emergency room. The doctor took an EKG, found nothing particularly abnormal (other than my premature ventricular contractions), but concluded, nonetheless, that I must have some sort of heart problem. "What else could it be?" he asked—as if I could shed some light on what was happening.

We drove home. I was constantly checking my pulse, and feeling as if everything around me was a dream. I saw a cardiologist in McAllen. He could find nothing wrong with my heart. He said the PVCs were stress related. He wanted to know what in my life was bothering me.

As the months passed, I began to feel even more isolated. I had leased a piece of land in Starr County with the excuse that it was for deer hunting. But more often than not, I went unarmed: a silent walker, following the most isolated paths, hiding from something that I had yet to identify.

Everywhere I went the world (my world) was being ripped apart. I was on that deer lease when I watched the adjacent ranch scraped clean of life. In a state of derealization, I saw that the four bulldozers—having violated the land across the fence—were now heading toward the tract I had leased. I drove to Rio Grande City and called the landowner. He apologized, saying that he *had* to take advantage of the government's land clearing program. He said that the bulldozers were going to leave a few windbreaks and that I could hunt the strips of brush that remained.

But it wasn't deer I was hunting. I was after quiet, unmolested earth—a place free from the blade and the plow. So life grew only darker.

When I wasn't working or trying to find a piece of land that had escaped the machines, I read. Voraciously. Hundreds of books. Psychology, biology, anthropology, philosophy, theology. It was a form of self-therapy: a way, perhaps, to find an answer to what had yet to coalesce into a definite question. But in that black period, I found that, for me, the best remedy was still the woods. So I hiked long hours down the canal bank (lined with hackberries, retamas, anaquas, mesquites) that ran east and west a hundred yards from my house. And I'd drive to Bentsen State Park, at the time still a mass of huge trees, and spend hours identifying birds and plants. I'd sit under the gigantic cedar elms and watch butterflies—red, purple, yellow, orange—as they lit on the soft, blue petals of *mejorana* shrubs and on the velvet crimson flowers of the *tulipan del monte.* As long as I was in the woods, I was okay.

Passions, after all, are the rudders that steer life on an even course. Without passions, life becomes fixed on mundane proclivities; people become automatons grafted to an endless, and meaningless, assembly line. Without passion there is nothing to hold onto when times get hard. For passions simultaneously focus and distract.

Had I not been passionate about nature, I would surely have been as directionless as a light skiff on a stormy sea. But the Brushlands pointed the way. I absorbed the natural world, concentrating on every idiosyncrasy within the woods, as if knowing instinctively that if I could take it all in, it too would absorb me.

My second son, Jason, was born in 1977 with an atrial septal defect. As much as we hoped it would be otherwise, deep down we knew that someday he would have to have open heart surgery.

Personal suffering shrinks to insignificance when your child feels pain. When we took Jason to have his first heart catheterization in Corpus Christi in 1979, I had to force my fears into the deepest recesses of my mind. In August of 1982 we traveled to Houston for Jason's second heart catheterization. Then I traveled alone to Boston, where my boy was operated on—September 30, 1982.

It took four and a half days to reach Boston, driving fourteen hours a day. By the time I reached my destination, I was exhausted. Jason and his mother arrived by plane the day I arrived by car. I had driven because we expected Jason's stay to be nearly a month, and I had the car packed for the duration.

I shall not forget the smile on Jason's little face as he walked down the corridor that led from the plane. At that moment I nearly broke. But I knew that no matter what, I must remain strong. Thank God, Jason survived the surgery; he now stands five inches taller than his old man.

On the road back from Boston to Mission, I asked God to show me a purpose in life. Like so many others, I had been swept up by the dictates of modern society. Too often, I had gauged self-worth by the material possessions surrounding me. But on that day as I drove south, I feel certain that God spoke to me. "You are a man of nature," He said. "Do not try to be what you are not. Your purpose will be revealed to you in time."

In 1985, I wrote a long story about a man who walks through the Brushlands, searching for peace, and wanting to experience the deep woods before they are all gone. Little did I know that my life would soon become nearly that story. In the interim, I would find consolation in nature.

One evening, as I lay back on the soft, leafy ground of an old resaca bank that centuries before had marked the path of the great Rio Grande,

I watched a family of pied-billed grebes make quick dives into the glassy water. Above me, a great-horned owl hooted melancholy notes from some deep woods perch; and to my right, a nutria ambled along the water's edge chewing a juicy morsel of some water plant. Sunset was less than an hour away.

"It will take time," I whispered. "A long time, perhaps." But I was sure now that my cure, and my *reason* for being, were in the Brushlands.

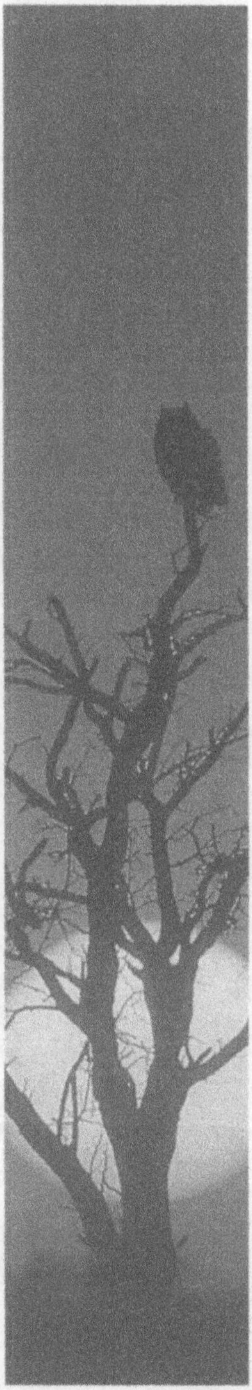

Part III
Fighting Back

Los Lobos Peninsula

Cold and misting. The first Saturday of February, 1986. We drive west—from Edinburg to Mission to Rio Grande City to Roma, leaving the cities and towns behind us. Through the gray nebula that settles amidst the leafless trees and holds the woods in splendid stillness, we enter the last vestige of deep South Texas brush as we traverse the northwestern fringes of Starr County then cross into Zapata County. With only a vague idea of what we're looking for, we journey on faith alone.

I have (the day before) accepted the job of Starr County reporter for McAllen's daily newspaper, the *McAllen Monitor.* My background is in biology, not journalism. But that is a plus, because I know what I want to concentrate on. Not that I am concerned, as I gaze into the frigid mist and at the band of blue clouds that push southward into Mexico. For the moment, I care only to find a quiet spot to park the Avion trailer that sits waiting to be moved back in Edinburg.

Of course, a quiet spot, for me, means the brush.

So we keep the Toyota pickup pointed north by northwest until we reach an isolated Texaco station about twenty-five miles south of the town of Zapata.

"Are there any places along Falcon Lake to park trailers?" I ask the attendant. She points to a dirt road three hundred yards behind us and says, "Down there, five miles."

The park looks perfect. Falcon Lake surrounds us on three sides. There are electricity and telephone (both will be needed for the job) and water is piped in from the town of Salineño. In the distance, we can see the giant gates of Falcon Dam sticking above the horizon like a megalithic gray fortress. The park's occupants are "Winter Texans": retirees escaping the frigid north. They fall in love with Norma. And since it's a package deal, I the other half, they accept me too.

"Cover commissioner's court, that sort of thing," *McAllen Monitor* editor Jack King had said the day before. So that was where I began. I plunged into my work like a hungry anhinga feeding atop the choppy waters of Falcon Lake. I began with election runoffs, commissioner's court, car wrecks, shootings, drug busts, and then branched into what I felt were more germane issues.

Six weeks into the job, I made the national news with a story on resident aliens abusing the welfare system. I also wrote a series of investigative stories on drug smuggling in South Texas. Of course, I began to write articles about the destruction of the Brushlands and about the pollution—agricultural chemicals, raw sewage, industrial solvents—afflicting the Rio Grande. Most of the features were picked up by Associated Press and other national news services. Exciting, yes. But all the while, I knew there was more to be done.

Since that day in 1969 when I watched the virgin brush north of El Ponderosita ripped from its roots and then consumed by flames, I had witnessed a seemingly never-ending rape of the land. Farmers and ranchers, quick to cash in on sundry government handouts, bulldozed and burned the Brushlands with impunity. No one had said, *Stop!* As if that were not enough, farmers have come to believe it is their right to poison the land with insecticides, defoliants, herbicides, and fungicides.

There are other problems as well.

The burning of thousands of acres of subsidized sugarcane turns the sky, during harvest season, a murky brown. The growers don't seem to care about the asthmatics, emphysema patients, and those with bronchial allergies who must endure the low-hanging clouds of smoke. But why should they? They've filled the skies with poisons for decades. And all the while, the destruction of the brush continues mercilessly. By 1986 the upland brush of deep South Texas was becoming almost as endangered as the whooping crane; and at least the great whoopers have people working on their behalf. Attempts were by then under way to save the unique riparian habitats lining the Rio Grande from Falcon Dam southeast to Brownsville, but creating a wildlife corridor along the river has not been an easy task. Damming and urbanization have already destroyed so much of the woodland buttressing the river that the future of the corridor looks bleak.

APRIL, 1986

Los Lobos Peninsula at the edge of Zapata County remains unharmed. The *jara* brush clusters along the water's edge, green pinnacles jutting out from the sand. It is in bloom, pale white flowers clumped at the ends of short, spindly branches that are tightly wrapped by slender, deeply toothed leaves. Mockingbirds whistle and chirp and stutter and yodel. Mourning doves and white-tipped doves counter with mellifluous notes, as smooth and tranquil as the white, pubescent clouds moving languidly overhead. Bees and butterflies fly hypnotically among plants of a hundred species. They light momentarily on the huisaches, now draped by thousands of marble-sized, yellow flowers, each one emitting an ambrosia fragrance that wafts serenely through the air. Then the insects, overwhelmed by the wealth of odors and colors, disperse to the cacti: nopal—yellow, red, orange; pitayas—purple and pink; and to the Berlandier's *alicoche,* carmine pink. The bees and butterflies scatter to the *hierba negra,* pink, and the *hierba dulce,* bleached white. They skim along the ground, dancing on the *hierba del venado,* bright yellow, and onto the Texas lantana, yellow and orange, and to the Texas frog fruit, white. Then it's back into the shrubs—whitebrush, sparkling white, and *vara dulce,* royal pink.

The lake (low in the spring of 1986) shimmers a bright aluminum hue from the edges of Los Lobos Peninsula to the banks of Nuevo Guerrero on the Mexican side. It is a time to write and a time to explore.

JUNE, 1986

The Winter Texans have left; they are back in Kansas, and Ohio, and Michigan, and other places far to the north. Norma and I are alone. Even Mr. and Mrs. Wolf, the park's owners, have headed for Riudoso, New Mexico, to play the horses and breathe mountain air. We explore the Old Falcon town site, about half a mile from the trailer park. It is usually underwater, but now the rock cisterns, rock foundations, and crumbled rock walls lie naked and muddied—like so many tombstones on a sandy beach. This was the town of Falcon. Like Old Guerrero across the lake, this ghost village has resurrected, if only momentarily.

An eerie feeling creeps over us as we sit quietly on the edge of one of the crusty cisterns. There was life here once. Children played, men and women labored and loved, and celebrated a quiet life in the only true valley in deep South Texas. They, most likely, had family in Guerrero, a few miles across the river. They would visit their friends and relatives. They would fish along the twisting banks of the Rio Grande. They would hunt the hills.

In the cistern—which over the decades has filled with rocks and silt but nonetheless still holds about five inches of water—I spot something dark and knurly. I put my hand into the brown water and gently lift the object.

"Look, it's an old horseshoe."

Norma turns to examine the artifact, her deep brown eyes reflecting the soft yellow light that skims off the lake from a setting sun. "Oh gosh, let me see it."

For some inexplicable reason she taps it on the cistern wall, and instantly it crumbles into a hundred pieces.

How does the saying go? *Don't cry over . . . broken horseshoes.*

AUGUST, 1986

We have taken to walking four miles every other day. My work as a journalist is something that happens "out there, in the world." Here, at Los Lobos, we have found another life. We have made a few new friends, too. Our Winter Texan friends will begin returning in early October. But I have met a fellow in Rio Grande City named Benito Treviño, Jr. He loves the woods as I do. He and his wife Toni come often to visit us at the trailer park. They accompany Norma and me on our walks. We talk of the Brushlands, and the animals and the birds—and cook fajitas and tortillas, and munch on picante, and drink iced tea.

I have also met Bill Matthews, the acting resident agent in charge at the U.S. Customs office at the Falcon Port of Entry. He is a fisherman, hunter, and photographer, and one hell of a narcotics agent.

OCTOBER, 1986

Schools of white bass bubble the lake's surface; ospreys sit atop the stubbly remains of water-logged mesquites; cormorants fly en masse to their roosts; the distant purr of a motorboat joins the sloshing water like *un enmienda* to a symphonic chorus.

Most of the Winter Texans are back: Colonel and Violet Young, Cleve and Goldy Buck, the Schwartzes, the Wellmans, the Wests—about twenty couples in all.

Norma and I have turned our four-mile walks into five- or six-mile hikes. We journey slowly, filling ourselves with a landscape of peaceful hills, the monte wrapping around us like a soft shearling blanket. Coyotes cross our path on almost every jaunt. Often, purple-gray clouds mushroom behind us as they rise over Mexico's mountains.

We never leave the Avion without binoculars. Ravens, mockingbirds, hawks, warblers, buntings, doves, killdeers, poorwills, pauraques, owls, gulls, curlews, woodpeckers, flycatchers, phoebes, dowitchers, thrashers, vireos, towhees—flutter, soar, and swoop above us.

Sometimes, on those crystal calm days when the lake's veneer lies unspoiled, Norma and I skirt the shore in my fourteen-foot canoe. We drift aimlessly, watching the land glide past us, each tiny inlet and small island a new wonderland to explore.

We'll glimpse beavers and raccoons sauntering along the sandy beach, or white-tailed deer scampering from tiny, mud-lined pools into dense thickets. Twice we spot a bobcat (one with a very yellow coat, the other gray and fat) following the faint game trails that meander between the jara shrubs and the giant old mesquites. Then there are the crayfish, turtles, and water snakes that crawl and slither from perches and hideouts into the depths. I am a child again. Or perhaps merely a real man, living a real life—reveling in nature's beauty and unconcerned with human works.

DECEMBER, 1986

At night, Norma and I sit outside the trailer and observe the stars. We play the satellite counting game. I always win, but maybe it's because she lets me. We listen to the night sounds of frogs, raccoons, owls, distant coyotes. I repeat to her the stories that Bill Matthews has told me about drug runners, shootouts, and the frustrations of working for an agency that often cares less about enforcing the law than about promoting individual agendas. But then Bill says "they're all like that": U.S. Customs, DEA, FBI, Border Patrol, BATF.

I've taken to spending a lot of time with Bill. Though only just turned fifty-eight, he looks ten years older, at least. He's battled obesity all his life but now he is thin and wrinkled, a long stay in a Houston hospital having brought his weight down to what a man standing five feet and nine inches ought to carry.

We've made several clandestine trips to the Rio Grande, where we've looked for signs of smuggling activity.

"It's everywhere," Bill says.

He kneels, then points to a cluster of footprints that have saturated a narrow trail.

"Look here. Tracks on top of tracks. These tracks going back to the river are on top of the tracks that went inland. Notice how the tracks coming back ain't as deep as the ones going away from the river. That's 'cause they'd already dropped off their load."

Bill stands, walks a few more yards toward the Rio Grande, then stoops and giggles.

"Sonuvabitch, look what we've got here. These are marijuana plants. Damn seeds drop out of the bundles and start growing right on the trail."

I've attended a few drug busts since becoming a reporter. Usually I follow the convoy of pickups and cars that swoops into a residence—cops jumping out, guns drawn, and rushing into the house, where they find (sometimes) a back room filled with bundles of coke or grass, and a closet where piles of money, in various denominations, lies carefully sorted. But now it's time to go in on the main wave: to be there on the front steps when the door gets shoved open and see firsthand the look of surprise on Mr. or Mrs. Mafioso.

We gather at the Falcon Port of Entry U.S. Customs office. USC, Border Patrol, Texas DPS, local Starr County sheriff's deputies. Fifteen guys, maybe. Laughing, telling dumb jokes, swapping lies, inquiring about one another's families, smoking cigarettes, walking outside then back inside, slapping shoulders and shaking hands, talking loudly, some quiet (too quiet), some noisy (too noisy).

"Now listen up, fellows."

Joe Garza—Texas DPS, short, graying sideburns, deep nasally voice—has just walked into the room.

"The C.I. just called Bill. He said the dope's there at the house. About eight hundred kilos of grass, and maybe another twenty keys of coke in a small brick building in the back."

Bill Matthews walks in. Joe pauses, and Bill nods for him to continue.

"Supposedly, there's nobody there right now—just some guys who muled the stuff up from the river last night. Word is they're not armed."

Bill steps forward. "Maybe ten or eleven fellows there. They can still slice you up bad with machetes, so watch out."

Clear, bright blue sky. Temperature about sixty degrees Farenheit. Ephemeral whiffs of cool air with barely enough strength to move the dry grass that sidelines the roadway. A perfect day to be in the woods.

And yet, there is a whole other world but a few miles from Los Lobos Peninsula.

We arrive.

I am the second man through the door—two steps behind Joe Garza. There are no "mules" at the house; the men have already hightailed it back to Mexico. There are only two *viejitos* sitting at the kitchen table, counting money; we later tabulate the amount at eleven grand. In a back room we find about one thousand pounds of marijuana, which is less than we had expected. We also find about forty pounds of cocaine.

Someone hands me a couple of rolls of color film. "Will you take pictures for us too?" he asks. "Okay," I say. So I dutifully begin photographing the evidence, wondering all the while how another drug story (they all begin to blend into a blurry series of numbers and pounds that readers find boring and become insensitive to) will be written.

Bill walks up and taps me on the shoulder.

"Not as much fun as sneaking around on the river, is it?" he asks.

"It's kind of exciting," I reply.

"Yeah, but down on the river we get to see all the birds, and the trees, and get to look at animal tracks, and check out fishing holes. You know what I mean."

The veteran lawman offers a wrinkled smile, then removes his thick trifocals and wipes them clean with a handkerchief. "Sure like to be down on the river today, cuttin' sign. We could've caught them mules early this morning, and got them to turn on their boss." He grins broadly. "And watched a hell of a sunrise."

FEBRUARY, 1987

I look forward to the weekend visits from my two boys, Nomar and Jason. Nomar is about to turn fourteen. Next month Jason will turn ten. We have decided to go exploring along the lake, which has begun to climb again. Since they were little, both boys have been taught woodsmanship. They know, instinctively, to walk quietly, to search for animal signs, to interpret the woods' discreet messages.

We have hiked for a mile, going north along the lake edge, looking for a suitable place to drop a line and then wait for an encounter with a choice black bass. A dry, northly breeze glides across the reservoir. A flock of black cormorants hug the water as they head northeast en route to a twig-studded inlet. To the west we can see plainly the Sierra Picachos—a gray, recumbent silhouette, as graceful and beautiful as a shapely woman.

"Hey Dad, how many fish do you think are in this lake?"

"Jason, there's no way Dad can know that. Geez, you ask the most unbelievable questions."

"I'm just asking for an estimate, Nomi. Huh Dad, how many fish?"

"I don't know, son. I guess it depends on the supply of food, the level of dissolved oxygen in the water, the amount of pollution."

A speedboat rushes across the water, churning a heavy, green wake in its path.

"Those guys out there sure are noisy," Nomar says.

"Messing up the fishing, too," says Jason.

"Can't they enjoy the lake without being so noisy?" Nomar insists.

"They're not smart enough," says Jason.

The speedboat fades into a black dot on the horizon, and the quiet returns.

I'd like to give my boys a hug, but they're getting too old for that. Still, I look at them and remember when they were little. I wish they could stay here with me. We could spend our days exploring the woods and fishing the lake. At night, we could go gigging for frogs, or just spend hours looking at the stars. But it can't be. And so I try to fill myself with the moments when they are here.

MARCH, 1987

Norma and I are at Bill and Martha Matthews' home at the government village, two miles from the Falcon Port of Entry. Bill has to leave in a few days to attend a training session in Arizona. Last year he attended a training session in Georgia. He left his double-barreled shotgun with me because he felt my investigative stories on organized crime might be getting a few people upset. He offers to leave the shotgun with me again. It's as if he doesn't feel comfortable going off. He thinks he should be around to give me some backup *just in case.* I'm the only journalist—as he puts it—who has had the *cajones* to go after the mafiosos.

"Thanks, Bill, but you know I've got that little .30-30 now, and that Ithaca twelve gauge."

"Yep, I know, it's just that—" Bill's words trail off as Norma and Martha reenter the living room from the kitchen.

I stand. It's time to go back to the Avion at Los Lobos, which sits right across a large inlet from the government village. Still, we have to drive clear around the peninsula to get to the park, and so it takes about twenty minutes to journey from one spot to the other. Bill and Martha accompany Norma and me outside. They stand in the yard and wave goodbye as we drive off. Martha will stay at the house while Bill is gone for nearly three weeks.

We have been at Los Lobos Peninsula for fourteen months. This place has become home. I don't think I ever want to leave. But we do have to go to McAllen now and then to visit the *McAllen Monitor's* main office. And naturally, I travel to Rio Grande City almost every day.

The month has turned windy and dry. In Rio Grande City dust swirls along the streets and forms a haze that clings stubbornly over the town. Everything has slowed down: a preface to the summer to come, when people in South Texas head indoors and wait for the cool temperatures of winter to return.

Norma and I have gone to visit Norma's parents in Sebastian, a tiny hamlet in southern Willacy County surrounded by miles of plowed fields. I check my recorder back at the Avion trailer and hear agent Tom Garcia's voice on the other end: *Call the U.S. Customs office at Falcon Dam as soon as possible.* I dial, and Tom Garcia answers the phone.

"What's going on, Tom?"

"I've got bad news, Arturo."

Instantly, even before he says it, I know.

"Uncle Billy died this morning."

"That can't be. How?"

"We don't have all the details yet. We think it was a massive heart attack. You know he'd been having those severe chest pains that were supposed to be from an esophageal hernia. Guess it wasn't so."

MAY, 1987

Strange how it's the same place. The sun still sets behind the Sierra Picachos, the cormorants still make their late afternoon flights across the lake, the spring flowers have come and gone, the deer still walk to the water's edge just before sunset to drink, the mockingbirds and doves still chirp and coo. But it is different.

The day after Bill died I wrote a piece in the *McAllen Monitor* about him. I called him a special man, because he was. But now, two months later, I still have not come to grips with his death. I see him standing in his front yard waving goodbye. Once when he called me, I taped the conversation. He wouldn't have liked that, but now I cherish that tape. Sometimes I'll just sit and listen to his baritone voice.

Norma and I still go on our walks. But now everything has turned gray. The green is gray, the brown is gray, the blue is gray. When I drive into Rio Grande City I start to think that Bill is really not gone, he's actually on some big undercover case. A car that looks like the one he used to drive will pass me. The windows are darkly tinted. I can't see the driver. But I know it's Bill. He's on the job; he's never left.

JULY, 1987

Norma and I have taken to spending a lot of time in the woods. We have found a hidden spot that even at noon on the hottest days remains enveloped by shade. We take a blanket to lay on the ground, some sandwiches, a thermos filled with iced tea, a couple of novels, our binoculars, a bird guide, and we stay secreted in this quiet place until the sun goes down. I still think about Bill a lot. I can't accept that he's gone. But Norma and the woods help me deal with the pain.

At night Norma and I regard with enchantment the lightning storms over the Mexican mountains. We watch the zigzagging laser pulses pounding the distant peaks and illuminating the lake, now filled with water. We also keep an eye out for wandering skunks.

One night, as we sit in the trailer looking out through the screen door, a family of striped skunks moseys up in search of food. One of the skunks stands on the trailer steps peering in at us. There's no way to close the door because it opens to the outside. Fortunately the lights in the trailer are out, so the skunk can't see us. After a few minutes, the skunks amble off. I smile and give thanks for a place like Los Lobos Peninsula.

AUGUST, 1987

I have been reassigned to the *McAllen Monitor*'s main office in McAllen. Part of me wants to stay, but a greater part needs to leave. I will spend a few more years working for the newspaper, but it will never be the same. Eventually, I will outgrow the *McAllen Monitor,* but for now I can only think of the times I've had here at Los Lobos. Norma wants to obtain a teaching certificate, and to do that we must return to a town. We don't know it yet, but a gift—from "Texas Heaven," as Norma puts it—will arrive next March. Of course, we will name him Matthew.

Paper against Steel

Dario Salinas, of the U.S. Soil Conservation Service, and I stood at the edge of a desert. The land lay trackless; the pale nakedness of caliche substrate and singed sterility from an unsympathetic sun had created a landscape as impotent as an emaciated steer.

"But it wasn't always like this," Dario said, the brim of his white straw hat pulled low against breeze-driven ringlets of caustic sand.

No bird lighted before us; no timid leaf attempted to break the hard, crusty ground. Yet, Dario explained, only a decade before there had been animals, large and small, roaming thorny thickets and sinewy ramaderos. Countless birds nested among lofty stands of mesquite, ebony, brasil, palo verde, and chapote trees. The sweet smell of huisache flowers filtered delicately through the air.

"But I guess no one cared about that," said Dario as we walked back to his pickup truck.

In all directions we saw nothing but bleak desolation. "We're lucky today," Dario explained, turning the pickup onto another side road that took us farther into the ranch country. "If the winds were really hard we'd have to flick on our headlights. Visibility would be only a few feet."

Dario Salinas pointed at two cows standing by the side of the road—nothing more than hide draped over bone. "We don't dare drive too close to those cows," he said. "They're too weak to move away from the truck." He added that a few days before he had blown his horn for a cow to move off the road, and the cow had simply collapsed. "We couldn't lift it up, so we just had to shoot it and then drag it off to burn." Dario paused. "I sure hope you write a good story about what you see here, today."

Thus began the first major news article about the rampant destruction of the South Texas Brushlands and the ensuing desertification of the region. "Genesis of a Desert" appeared in the *McAllen Monitor* on May 11, 1986.

Reaction was immediate, its nature of course depending on the political bent of the reader. Salinas's boss at the SCS office in Rio Grande City was livid. Bureaucrats, after all, spend most of their time trying to convince their superiors that all goes well. Many farmers and ranchers were also angered. The article did not speak well of the cowboy-caretaker myth. But there were many others who wrote or called to say that an article addressing the greed that drives many landowners to abuse the earth was long overdue.

In the late 1960s and early 1970s, the price of grain skyrocketed to $7.50 a bushel. Many South Texas landowners saw dollar signs and began bulldozing the upland brush. But with no irrigation available, farmers recklessly depended on the area's scant rainfall to provide needed moisture. The artificially high grain prices eventually fell, and farmers quickly abandoned the ruined land. By 1986 northwestern Starr County alone had lost over fifteen thousand acres of virgin brush. As Dario Salinas described it, "The land was valuable habitat for deer and other animals. But now it's just a desert."

In May of that year, South Texas had experienced six months of drought. Not unusual for the region; South Texas has been called a place of perpetual dryness interrupted by an occasional monsoon. Many ranchers compounded the problem by maintaining poor range conditions. "When it does rain and there's plenty of grass," Dario said, "the ranchers overstock their land with cattle. Soon the excess cattle overgraze, and the land deteriorates rapidly."

The soil conditions in Starr and Hidalgo counties had plummeted to the point that *any* substantial rainfall would do more harm than good. "It's a vicious cycle now," Dario lamented. "If we get a hard rain these desert areas will be wrecked even further by water erosion."

Nonetheless, the destruction continued unabated. Bulldozers that snapped large trees as easily as a man breaks a toothpick and giant, iron-clawed rootplowing machines that disgorged the earth of roots and undergrowth as if they were lions ripping the guts from their prey devoured tens of thousands of acres of brush. Compounding the outrages, when crops were planted, airplanes and tractors came to spray tons of insecticides, herbicides, fungicides, and defoliants.

Surprisingly, some people in the Soil Conservation Service who should have been on the side of Brushland preservation seemed more aligned with those who wanted all the brush cleared. As they saw it, only those plants that "serve man's needs" have value. Plants or animals that do not benefit people need not exist.

In South Texas the mesquite is the best illustration of this phenomenon. It has been called a "moisture-robbing plant." But what that really means is that the mesquite robs from profits, *robs from the potential to make money.* In the broad scheme of Nature, ironically, the mesquite robs far less moisture than do people who pollute lakes, rivers, and oceans or who poison the air. Who then is the great thief? In fact, most Brushland plants—those that do not fit into human profit schemes—hold the rank of "pest." Only the prickly pear cactus and some of the native grasses are considered worth keeping since they are used for cattle feed. Discover, however, that mesquite holds the cure for cancer or some other disease, and—miracle of miracles—the scourge of the Brushlands will lose the title of moisture-robbing plant; instead it will be considered a valuable commodity.

In Zapata County I saw how quickly land erodes after being cleared. A rancher bulldozed about three hundred acres on the south side of the county road ten miles east of where we lived. But the north side of the road must have belonged to someone else; it remained a diverse consortium of Brushland plants. A small creek, which filled with water after heavy rains, intersected the road leading from the cleared land into the wooded land. After a late summer downpour the creek on the cleared side of the road expanded to over five times its original width within an hour of the rain. But on the side of the road where brush remained, the creek stayed narrow.

A week later the rains came again—the water spilling unencumbered across raw earth and dissolving the soil like acid burning exposed flesh. The creek widened, then broke into a half-dozen panicked rivulets: the water searching hysterically for more land to consume. Bushel baskets of mud collapsed from the sides of the fanning creeks; the land looked as if a giant had drawn a huge rake across it. Yet on the other side of the road, where a thousand shrubs and trees stood quietly and undisturbed, the ground stayed motionless.

Whoever bulldozed that land in Zapata County showed profound ignorance. But as my first article had revealed, the motives for clearing land in other areas were based solely on greed. In an article I published in the July 17, 1988, issue of the *McAllen Monitor,* others made the point even clearer.

Gonzalo Guerra, who headed the Federal Crop Insurance District program in Hidalgo County, said that some farmers cleared the upland brush not because they intended to raise crops but because they wanted to take advantage of the insurance payments. In deep South Texas throughout the 1970s and early 1980s, unscrupulous farmers cleared land knowing that nothing would grow. They intended only to collect federal insurance money when the crop "failed."

Noe Garza from the Edinburg office of the SCS agreed: "These farmers and ranchers farm the [government] programs and not the crops." He added that farmers often divide their business into many parts in order to manipulate the government's subsidy and insurance supports. "There's one farmer in McCook," Garza said, "who collected over $400,000 in farm subsidies in 1987, and there's a large ranch in Willacy and Kenedy counties that collected over $800,000." Indeed, U.S. Department of Agriculture figures for 1995 indicate that farmers living in Bee, Brooks, Cameron, DeWitt, Goliad, Hidalgo, Jim Wells, Karnes, Kleberg, Live Oak, San Patricio, and Willacy counties—which form only a portion of South Texas—collected nearly $24 million in subsidies and other farm programs; Americans dish out some $11 billion annually for farm subsidies.

Curiously, these farmers and ranchers who take billions of subsidy and crop insurance dollars annually are often the same people who blast the welfare recipient. But in South Texas welfare goes in substantial quantities to farmworkers who are not paid a living wage, thus making welfare for the farmworker another form of subsidy for the farmer.

In 1994, a farmer in Willacy County was convicted of abusing the government's crop programs. In 1996 five farmers, all of whom were involved in major farming operations in Hidalgo and Starr counties, were accused of falsifying harvest amounts in order to collect federal insurance and disaster payments. Two of the farmers pleaded guilty.[1] Officials with the U.S. Farm Service Agency, which administers crop insurance payments, have suggested that abuse of the farm support system may be substantial. According to officials in the U.S. Department of Agriculture, farmers defraud American taxpayers by as much as $30 million annually. In 1996, the federal crop insurance program was reorganized (though not enough, as far as many are concerned) in order to thwart attempts by farmers to misuse the system—for system, read *American taxpayers.* Between 1991 and 1993, Hidalgo County farmers alone collected $18.9 million in crop insurance payments.

Of course, all this makes nonsense of advertisements claiming that American food is cheap. In fact, Americans pay dearly for their food. They pay through the front door at the supermarket; they pay through the back door via farm supports. And then what of the money that Americans spend acquiring medical care after becoming ill from eating food laced with pesticides, herbicides, defoliants, and fungicides—or after they are directly exposed to pesticide drift, or from drinking water contaminated with agricultural chemicals? Then don't forget the costs of cleaning the water, the soil, and the air when these become saturated with farm chemicals.

By the late 1980s the effects of desertification in deep South Texas had reached significant proportions. Sand dunes covered fence posts along many county roads. Segments of highways like U.S. Highway 281 north of Edinburg lay periodically beneath a layer of sand that might be as much as several inches thick. In order to document the extent of this desertification, I published an article in the *McAllen Monitor* on April 30, 1989, entitled: "Loss of Ground Cover is Taking its Toll." In the article, I quoted Juan Renteria of the Edinburg SCS office. At first, Renteria was reluctant to talk. But later, after realizing that my article would not threaten him directly, he agreed to discuss the growing deserts in South Texas. "We've been urging farmers to put [permanent] wind strips to keep the soil down, but we can only suggest it," Renteria said. He added, however, that few farmers seemed interested in employing sound wind erosion techniques.

For some time the most popular method for preventing soil erosion in South Texas had been to maintain large dirt clods in cultivated fields, the idea being that the relatively smaller surface area of large clods inhibited erosion. The practice, however, proved myopic at best.

Renteria explained: "The McCook area [where some of the most extensive land clearing has occurred] is very sandy, and you're not going to get big dirt clods. The only way to keep down erosion there is to have wind strips, or to leave a cover crop." He added that none of the farmers in the McCook area had expressed interest in wind strips or cover crops.

But again, why should they? The dry-land farmers cultivated government programs, not crops. If they had a productive season then all the better. But the emphasis had never been on producing grain, cotton, or corn. The focus had always been on squeezing every last available dollar from Uncle Sam's coffers.

In McCook and other dry-land farming areas, farmers had no interest in establishing wind strips that, though preserving the soil, would inhibit the amount of subsidized land. There also seemed to be a skewed mindset among some farmers, who viewed land with cover vegetation as somehow less pleasing than barren land. This incredible logic created dust storms—when the dry southeast winds blew in February and March—that brought visibility down to less than a quarter-mile in the Starr County hamlets of La Reforma and San Isidro. When dry northers kicked tons of exposed soil into the sky the towns of Mission, McAllen, and Edinburg were enveloped with a nearly opaque conglomerate of sand and powdered clay.

Soil erosion in deep South Texas had become so extensive in the late 1980s that the National Wildlife Federation called the Rio Grande Valley one of the most severely wind-eroded areas in the United States. The NWF research concluded that an average of fifteen tons of soil *per acre* was being lost annually in many parts of the region.

Yet despite the research conclusions, and in plain view of miles of rolling sand dunes and dust-laden skies, some bureaucrats still wanted to look the other way, so great was their allegiance to the very interests they were supposed to regulate. "This [the drought and sand dunes] is an abnormal situation," maintained Richard Whittington of the Agriculture Stabilization and Conservation Service in Edinburg. Whittington angrily denounced those who were trying to make an issue of the desertification of South Texas. He said that if it were not for the ongoing drought, no one would be concerned about the sand dunes.

But as much as some bureaucrats wanted to overlook or even hide the problems of wind erosion, many private citizens were watching, and they were willing to speak out.

"Whittington doesn't [know] what's going on," said Benito Treviño, Jr. of Rio Grande City. The Starr County conservationist added that for too long, government agencies in South Texas had addressed water erosion and practically ignored wind erosion, which Treviño claimed was the greater issue.

Whittington countered that the 1985 Food and Agricultural Act addressed both the topics of "highly erodible land" and "wetlands." He said that in order to participate in government subsidy programs, farmers and ranchers must present a "plan of action" for erodible land. "[Farmers] have got to comply with the law, or they won't be able to participate in the [subsidy] programs," Whittington said.

But an important piece of information had been left out. In South Texas, many ranchers and farmers received subsidies despite the fact that their land continued to erode. How did they do it? By manipulating the system. The 1985 Food and Agricultural Act had a catch. Land that had a history of planting could qualify for the subsidy program, and hundreds of farmers took advantage of that clause because their land had been farmed for at least a decade.

"Actually much of that land should never have been put into cultivation," Whittington admitted.

In the April 30, 1989, *McAllen Monitor* article, John Martin of the Frontera Audubon Society warned that continued clearing of land in northern Mexico and South Texas would create a vast desert. He added that a South African biologist, considered an expert on deserts, concluded after visiting the McCook area that the extensive erosion and loss of habitat had the makings of another Sahara Desert. Martin questioned the logic behind the government's "financial promotion," via subsidies and insurance, to farmers who did not conserve their land.

Recent Congressional moves to end farm subsidies and other agricultural supports, which encouraged farmers and ranchers to clear habitat, have perhaps come too late for much of South Texas. On the twentieth anniversary of Earth Day, I was asked to help plant a tree at the University of Texas-Pan American in Edinburg. As students and faculty gathered around to watch the ceremony, I could not help but think that elsewhere, possibly within only a few miles, hundreds of trees and shrubs were being smashed to the ground by some bulldozer, their roots simultaneously shredded by a rootplow. The degradation of the Brushlands had reached a point where only two paths were plausible. Somehow, the customs, traditions, and habits of the people who had for so long looked at nature as nothing more than an economic commodity would have to change. If they did not adopt a caring ethic, a deep sense of reverence for God's creations, then they would surely watch it all crumble away, too late realizing that they were destroying themselves as they destroyed the things around them.

El Río Grande

Thousands of fish—like flickering pearls strewn haphazardly on the sandy banks and algae-covered rocks—lay rotting. Carp, blue and yellow catfish, needle-nose and alligator gar, black and white bass—as if the mighty Rio Grande, in a moment of extreme duress, had suddenly vomited its contents onto the land. There were no immediate explanations. The fish simply floated to the top, as lifeless as the sandstone forming narrow fords across the water.

The river had become a foreign place, as distant as the years that separate the present from the past. I swatted at persistent insects and smelled the stench of decaying flesh, all the while trading glances between the silver sheen of fly-infested water and the tall *sauz* and *olmos* trees that bent lazily into an arch from both sides of that formidable trench traversed by the Rio Grande. But it wasn't always like this.

We sit quietly on the banks of the Rio Grande—Uncle Bill, cousins Mark and Dora Inez, and Papagrande and I—watching the water inch its way past us, listening to the meow of green-headed towhees and eating tortillas de harina folded over huevos rancheros. A blue sky overhead; a gentle breeze blowing across the green grass; our fishing lines marked by bobbing corks; a string of catfish submerged in the clear water.

I hadn't noticed the blond-haired man approaching. He stood nervously next to me for a moment before saying something about a crop duster dumping a cloud of poison into the river earlier in the afternoon.

"Why would they do that?" I asked.

"To get rid of whatever insecticide remains in their tanks," the man replied. "That way they can charge their customer for using the whole amount."

The blond-haired man stroked his red-bearded face with the back of his freckled hand, then said, "They never leave the river alone, you know. The poisons wash into it, and the water turns orange-brown when the raw sewage floats down from the villages on the Mexican side."

In the grassy meadow, Mark, Dora Inez and I sit quietly behind Uncle Bill and Papagrande. Papagrande has just thrown out another line. And all the while he reminds Uncle Bill that it was his rod and reel that hooked the great gar that made the world's record book.

"Yes, but I was the one who brought it in," Uncle Bill says, grinning.

"And it's your name in the book," Papagrande says, sorely.

Uncle Bill fumbles for another cigarette, and Papagrande does the same. I walk to a shaded area fifty feet farther back, then sit under the sagging limbs of a hunched-back sauz to escape the smell of tobacco that will overshadow the fragrance of the woods until both men have tossed their spent smokes into the water.

Papagrande and Uncle Bill are still discussing the great fish. But I do not remember much about the world's record alligator gar—other than a dim recollection of the giant beast hanging from Mark and Dora Inez's backyard swing, the mighty tail dragging the ground, the long snout protruding several feet above the crossbar.

An hour passed, and a Texas game warden arrived. He looked tired and disinterested. He surveyed the holocaust, then walked back to his car and retrieved a couple of jars which he would use to take water samples.

The woman who had called me about this June, 1986, fish kill, and who had been standing next to me all the while, and who was furious, and who said the Rio Grande had become a thousand-mile toxic dump, chided the game warden for being so late. The game warden did not comment, other than to say that he had been up all night looking for gill netters on Falcon Lake.

The woman—whose name, I had learned, was Dina Saldaña and who owned a small piece of land along the river—was not impressed. She said she and her husband were ready to move from this area; perhaps they would find a place farther north in Zapata County. She had seen enough of river pollution.

It is nearing noontime. The sun has warmed the day enough to make it uncomfortable. Besides, the fish have sought deeper and cooler water, and Papagrande and Uncle Bill have a string that now hangs with at least forty pounds of succulent catfish.

"Time to go home," Uncle Bill says.

But I have no desire to leave. Home is noisy and crowded. Here the great kiskadees and ladder-backed woodpeckers resonate calls weave through the deep eclipse of tall palo blancos, sauz and olmos trees, from which dangle long, spiraling strands of gray Spanish moss. I follow dark, serpentine tunnels and find enchanted leaf-covered hollows in the deepest woods. Strange sounds echo from phantoms and other creatures that live beyond eyesight. I walk quietly, trying desperately but often unsuccessfully to avoid the brittle leaves. My ears strain to catch the faint rustle of brush that forewarns of stalking beasts on both sides of that curtain of trees and vines that frames my path.

An indigo snake, six feet long or better, slithers across the tree-shrouded tunnel, and I wait to let it pass. Then I notice something small and reddish-tan lurking in the shadows to one side. The animal is catlike, but not housecatlike. It's sinuous body hugs the ground; its tightly arched back and rigid legs tell me that it waits to pounce or flee.

A mosquito buzzes my face, and since I am young and inexperienced, I twitch. The beast springs backward at my clumsiness, then in a strange loping stride disappears into the entanglement of trees, shrubs, and vines that quickly confuses my eyes . . .

• • •

Having filled the two small jars with water, the game warden placed both on the hot hood of his car. He walked back and stared at one of the dead carp, removing his hat and wiping the sweat off his brow with the sleeve of his shirt.

"You need to take some fish, put them on ice, and then let the lab analyze them," I suggested.

"Ain't got no ice," the warden says. "Got no place to carry the fish, neither."

"And maybe you'd best remove the jars from the hood of your car. The heat"—I wanted to make it clear that leaving the jars on the hood was poor technique—"might destroy whatever poisons or bacteria, or anything else that might be in the water."

The warden grunted but walked back to his car, lifted the jars off the hood, and placed them in the trunk—which was probably as hot as the hood. I made no further comment.

Two days later, I met a couple of employees from the Texas Water Commission at a place called Falcon Heights. They had come to take water samples. But they did not sample the water in the Rio Grande where the fish kill had occurred; they sampled the water in Falcon Reservoir. At the same time the Texas Parks and Wildlife Department—assuming that the Texas Water Commission had tested the Rio Grande's water—disposed of the two water-filled jars that the game warden had collected at the fish kill.

When I wrote in the newspaper about the bumbling bureaucracies, both agencies quickly blamed each other, and then when that didn't work, they did what all bureaucracies do when caught being negligent: they denied. The Texas Water Commission promptly issued a statement that the fish had died from oxygen deprivation. Of course, it was impossible to know this since they had collected no data. I also learned that the diagnosis of oxygen deprivation is commonly used to explain massive fish kills. I began to wonder how many times that excuse had been employed in order to cover for less than scrupulous work.

A few months later, on October 14, 1986, I published an article on the pollution of the lower Rio Grande. As it turned out, this was the first news story in South Texas to address the great river's problems. The story was picked up by the Associated Press, and that brought national attention to a river that had largely been ignored.

In researching the article, I learned that the sixteen Texas counties bordering the Rio Grande from El Paso County to Cameron County have an inordinately high incidence of liver cancer. The cancer rate mimics the disease conditions in Third World countries. The one common denominator is the Rio Grande. In the story, I quoted Dr. Irina Cech, a hydrologist at the University of Texas Health Science Center in Houston. She suggested that agricultural toxins and raw sewage contamination in the Rio Grande might play a significant role in the etiology of those cancers.

This was information that citizens wanted to know, that politicians wanted to avoid, that the business community wanted suppressed. Other articles appeared. But the Rio Grande received no mercy. Every U.S. border community saw the river as simply an obstacle between it and the burgeoning Mexican trade. The river was a nuisance, an impediment, something to be bridged and then forgotten.

The only real attempt made in deep South Texas to save anything associated with the Rio Grande belonged to that ambiguous government project called the Rio Grande Valley Wildlife Corridor, a consortium of federal, state, and private refuges of which one, the Lower Rio Grande Valley National Wildlife Refuge, was specifically linked to the Rio Grande. The enterprise was heavily touted as a great conservation effort; the unique habitats lining the Rio Grande from southeast of Brownsville northwest to Falcon Dam would be saved via a long corridor edging the water, providing habitat for birds like chachalacas and green jays and for small mammals like the ocelot and jaguarundi. But there were problems from the start. Those who conceived of a continuous wildlife corridor skirting the river did not envision the exponential growth of the region. Nor did they take into account the mindset of the people who live along the border.

From its inception, the Rio Grande Valley Wildlife Corridor was besieged by an ever increasing number of colonias and other developments, which flooded the "unspoiled" woods with feral dogs and cats that chased and ate the small mammals and birds for which the habitat had ostensibly been set aside. And despite token efforts by the larger communities to placate the U.S. Fish and Wildlife Service by providing portals allowing animals to cross beneath roadways servicing brand new international bridges—which span out from the U.S. side of the river into Mexico like curling fingers enticing the Mexicans to come and spend their booty—the Corridor has remained nothing more than a hodgepodge of trash-ridden woodlands. It will never be interconnected, and it is *not* the private domain of the animals and plants.

The government—the U.S. Fish and Wildlife Service, the Border Patrol, U.S. Customs, the DEA, the Tick Riders, and even secret U.S. Army units working in what some proclaim is a blatant violation of federal laws—roam the Corridor at will. As do Mexicans and Central and South Americans, who strap themselves to inner tubes or straddle inflated plastic garbage bags and then head for better times in the United States. People entering the country illegally promptly abandon their flotation devices once they reach the soft sands of the American side. In many places the banks of the great river lie buried beneath growing deposits of plastic bags, inner tubes, makeshift rafts, and an assortment of refuse that might include discarded clothing, bailing wire, broken furniture, and even abandoned bags of marijuana. Naturally, the woodlands of the Corridor have also become a sanctuary for drug smugglers.

So much for animal privacy. But even that is not all. Most of the distinctive habitats that lined the Rio Grande from below Brownsville to Falcon Dam (sabal palm groves, barretal slopes, Montezuma bald cypress stands) were unique because the river was *alive.* Great floods immersed the lands along the Rio Grande, saturating the ground with water, carving channels, and dumping organic matter in inundations that produced a true wonderland of riparian habitat. Until the dams—Falcon Dam, Amistad Dam, Anzalduas Dam—broke the river's spirit. The Rio Grande's life was squelched. The sprawling floods became a thing of the past. The underground water supplies dried up. The effusion of natural fertilizers came no more. When the river was tamed, the unique habitats were denied their lifeblood.

In Bentsen State Park west of Mission, and in Santa Ana National Wildlife Refuge south of San Juan—locales where tall ebonies, cedar elms, palo blancos, and sauz once reached skyward—the habitats changed. Now, instead of walking beneath vast expanses of shade, one hikes trails lined with small trees, grass, and woody shrubs. The decaying trunks of the great trees remind one of how it used to be. So much for unique habitats.

And there is still more. Many South Texas natives—people who have been shut out of the land by the big ranches that nudge the northern boundaries of the Rio Grande Valley—considered the great river their private domain. Traditions and laws that date back to the Treaty of Guadalupe Hidalgo, which followed the U.S. war against Mexico in the mid-1800s, gave the people virtually unrestricted access to the Rio Grande via established trails. For decades the sequestered citizens living along the river sought a moment of freedom at the water's edge. Now, however, even those lands are off limits. No Trespassing signs cramp the people of the lower Rio Grande Valley like the hard edges of a steel vise. Signs on the south, along the river, proclaim that the land belongs to the U.S. government. Signs on the north proclaim that the land belongs to the big ranches. Many people, especially the descendants of those who lost their lands to Anglo terrorism and politics, view both the government and the owners of the big ranches as thieves. They believe the ranches to the north were stolen in the last century. Now they feel that the Rio Grande has been taken as well. With no access to the land or river, and with no way to connect to nature, how long does anyone believe that the status quo will be maintained? Not long, I suggest. Old men grown weary of life's battles can always find contentment in their memories of how it used to be. The young, unfortunately, cannot enjoy that luxury. They will either have to change the direction the world has taken or endure the void it has created.

Lost Islands of the Rio Grande

We have come to float the river. From the concrete footings of Falcon Dam to the wooded serenity of Santa Margarita—a village that has escaped the wrath of economic growth and urban sprawl and that lies, like a cherished heirloom, on the banks of the somnolent Rio Grande. We have come to see brown jays, Muscovy ducks, yellow-headed parrots, and red-billed pigeons. We have come to gaze at the layered mats of emerald woods that suspend lazily into the river's green waters. We have come to partake of silence, of the serene calm that is penetrated by nothing more than the gossamer calls of birds and rhythmic swishes of canoe paddles.

The sun has emerged in the east; its blue-white light ripples like a thousand sparkling diamonds across the water. In the earlier predawn darkness, when we drove through Rio Grande City, I insisted on stopping off at a *panaderia* to collect a few bagfuls of *pan dulce,* Mexican sweet bread. "But we'll be wasting time," said one of the bunch—David Porras, Larry Ditto, David Blankenship, Jon Andrew, Benito Treviño, and Larry Clubb—now devouring the bread I bought like starved concentration camp prisoners just released from their tormentors. A nice bunch; they left me with one *mollete.*

Perhaps for some it is simply a canoe ride. But for others, it is much more. Three canoes. Three crews. Benito, Larry Clubb, and I. David Porras and Jon. Larry Ditto and David Blankenship. No leaders, no followers. No groups, actually. Each man journeys alone, lost in his own thoughts and reflecting on this trip in his own way.

"It feels like we're somewhere along the Amazon," somebody says in a low voice. "Mmm," someone else agrees. Already, the loud talk and laughs that circled us at the base of Falcon Dam have been sucked away. We canoe in awe. No one escapes the powerful message that transcends the serenity and harmony and that—strangely—seems so out of place.

Which world do we belong to? Out there, not more than ten miles away, cars and trucks filled with more concentration camp prisoners speed along U.S. Highway 83. The paved corridors connect one camp (McAllen, Rio Grande City, Laredo) to another. The prisoners' minds remain blissfully empty or filled with useless minutiae. Either way, they too have forgotten where they came from.

We see the first red-billed pigeon. Paddles instantly retreat from the water as we lie motionless, allowing the land to drift past us. It's been only twenty minutes since we launched, but it is amazing how quickly the mind begins to repair itself when allowed to reenter its home.

There are two red-bills. They do not seem to care that we have edged beneath the giant Montezuma bald cypress where they perch. Larry Ditto, the wildlife photographer, wants a picture. Larry Clubb, the newspaper photographer, wants a picture of Ditto taking a picture. The rest of us take photos too: snap shots imprinted sharply onto the visual cortex of the occipital lobe, then transferred and etched delicately in places not far removed.

I breathe deeply as the river pulls the land slowly around us. And just ahead, I spot the first island. For an instant, a Huckleberry thought glimmers. The island draws nearer.

This stretch of the Rio Grande between Falcon Dam and the city of Roma in Starr County has many islands. Someone, I am sure, has taken the time to count exactly how many. A biologist, probably. The islands were counted, then measured, the plant diversity on each island cataloged, the fluctuating water depths plotted, the soil analyzed. A graduate student, perhaps. Or some desperate college professor or government bureaucrat looking to publish—something. A good topic. A publishable topic. Very scientific. About as sterile as the inside of an autoclave. And if there were any animals roaming about, then they too would be subject to investigation. Tagged. Radio collared. Numbered. Painted. Damn good science.

I've often thought that any biologist who places a transmitting collar around an animal should be required to wear a radio collar as well for as long as the poor beast is forced to carry the confounded contraption.

Stop it, Longoria . . . push those frustrations aside.

The island now approaches to within five feet. We elect not to stop. *Leave it alone.* On all sides, the island's foliage elbows heavily into the water, making it impossible to land. We can only glimpse the dark padding of sticks and leaves concealing the soil beneath. Another world, unmolested and mysterious, awaits but a few feet away, yet completely out of reach.

We spot a Muskovy duck on a small log, watching us. It drifts on by, as we seem to stand still. It must be an illusion. Where is the human mass that is supposed to be gathering at the water's edge on the Mexican side just waiting to swim across? And where are the narcotics smugglers, their trucks idling on both banks, one truck full of dope, the other truck waiting to be loaded with the weed or powder? Not today, thank God.

But it does go on, the illegal entry of both people and narcotics. They arrive and cross mostly at night. Those who enter the United States illegally usually choose places farther downriver because this area, and a few other choice spots along the Rio Grande, belong almost exclusively to the narcotics traffickers.

This would not be a good place to be at night. The trees and shrubs and vines collect into a green web that restricts visibility to no more than ten feet; and the only way from the river inland comes via narrow walking paths that meander around scores of perfect ambush sites. I have been here in the darkness enough times to know that death lurks here after sunset.

I spot a trail leading to the water's edge. It looks so innocent, and tame. But it was a trail very much like the one now sliding past us that I and a team of U.S. Customs agents walked one dark night—farther downriver—a few years before.

We arrived at dusk. A mural of green, brown, and black woodland and tiger-stripe camouflage. M-16s, Steyr AUGs, and short-barreled Remington 870 pump shotguns. Starlight goggles and scopes. Pocket-sized two-way radios. Olive-drab canteens. Combat knives. And frayed, wool blankets slung over shoulders for the long hours on cold, wet earth, waiting.

We entered a thin trail. Within seconds it was as if the light from all the universe had been siphoned into some forbidding hole from which no one dared retrieve it. The blackness was both our friend and enemy. Only the man at the front of this pack train of automatic rifles and sawn-off shotguns wore night eyes. I, among the less fortunate, could not see the man in front of me, though he was less than three feet away. Those of us who walked in the darkness saw only with our ears; the sounds of the man directly in front were all each of us had to follow.

Suddenly, something stung my face just below my eyes. It was only a branch, but like most of the branches on most of the trees in deep South Texas, it was plumed with needle-sharp thorns. Finally, we reached the water, and as if a thick, velvet curtain had suddenly risen before us, the stars broke out in a million bright pinholes across the heavens. The leader, the man with the night eyes, directed us to our hiding places: our cocoons. We settled onto the cold sand like larvae awaiting metamorphosis.

By ten o'clock, the wintery night had crawled over the river, like a predatory ghoul in search of its next victim. I did not know to bring a blanket, so I was cold and wet. But at least a pair of starlight goggles was produced from someone's bag and loaned to me, so I passed the frigid hours scanning the opposite bank, waiting for the truck that was supposed to drive up to a road that married the river on the Mexican side.

We waited. And waited.

On the Mexican side, two or three miles away, a radio tower's red beacon pulsed lethargically. Hypnotically. I watched and waited and dreamed of places far away, in both time and distance.

Abruptly, there was a sound. Metallic.

I pressed the starlight goggles to my eyes and felt my quickened pulse beating into the muscles of my face. A truck was driving down the bank to the water's edge on the Mexican side; a smaller pickup truck followed it. Earlier, I had been handed a Smith & Wesson .357 Magnum revolver, and then told not to use it . . . "unless." I was also told that the traffickers would have scouts waiting on the American side. Now the thoughts—those obsessive ruminations that rip apart jagged pieces of quivering nervous tissue—began to take hold. Perhaps the scouts watched but a few yards away, hidden in trees or dug in like badgers in the sand. They would surely be armed, with 12 gauge shotguns with barrels that looked like the entrance to Carlsbad Caverns when held closely to the face. Or they might have AR-15s or AK-47 look-alikes. Either way, my little *(my tiny)* .357 with its puny four-inch barrel would be poor medicine if the "unless" happened.

My goggles stayed glued to my eyes. Two men were taking something out of the back of the pickup. They placed the package on the sand. They unfolded it slowly, laying it out carefully. Then they connected a simple air pump to it and began filling what I realized was a raft.

More waiting. Chills. Ruminations.

The raft sat unattended as the men, now five in all, stood alongside the truck. Two were carrying FN-FAL battle rifles. That is what the Mexican Army uses, but those guns are also available on the U.S. side at hefty prices. The FN-FAL fires the NATO 7.62 round, commercially known as the .308 Winchester. It carries at least twenty rounds and can deliver them with amazing accuracy and astonishing punch out to about five hundred yards. My Smith & Wesson continued to shrink. My ruminations told me that it had become a rubber-band gun.

The five men were now walking to the rear of the large truck. One man climbed inside. Bundles begin appearing—tossed from the truck to the men on the ground in a sort of water brigade sequence. The last man placed the bundles into the raft. The metamorphosis had begun.

The men slid the raft into the water, then two smugglers manned the boat across the river. One seemed to be operating an electric motor, but the engine was so quiet that I could not hear its purr. The raft trudged slowly, barely making a wake.

More waiting. And freezing. Hours had past since I had last seen anyone. The agents I had accompanied into this black hole were supposed to be hiding nearby. But what if I was alone—with a rubber-band gun?

The raft scraped solidly on the U.S. side. Both men jumped out and began unloading the bundles. The night had become coffin quiet, save for the muffled crunching of bundles stacked atop bundles. Within a minute, the raft was unloaded; the two men stood alongside, one massaging his back while the other reached into the water to wash his face silently.

Then from the right came the rhythmic sounds of footsteps traversing damp earth. Three figures were walking toward me—or at least it looked as if they were. One carried a pump shotgun; the second and third looked unarmed.

"Parate," someone yelled from the brush to my right. *"Federales! Americano!"*

Instantly, the two men who had escorted the raft from the Mexican side leaped into the water. The other three men who had walked up appeared temporarily disoriented. Then, like a lightning bolt, hell reached across the blackness from the other side.

There is no time frame between a rifleshot and the slamming of bullet into trees or earth or flesh. The events are too nearly simultaneous for the mind to register any distinction between them. You either duck to safety as bullets impact nearby or you drop involuntarily.

The three men who had just walked past me had managed to burrow their own tunnels into the brush, but I sensed that they were not seeking distant lands alone. English-speaking voices were yelling for them to stop. But I was much more concerned with the FN-FALs thunder, now matched by the high-pitched bangs coming in considerable volume from the M-16s and Steyr AUGs. Amazingly, no one was hit, although the large truck and pickup on the Mexican side looked as if they had gone through something akin to a hailstorm.

Then it was over. The last echo from the last volley succumbed to the soundproofing effects of thousands of plants jammed tightly against the water. The action lasted no more than ten or twelve seconds. It lasted forever.

Hours later—as an impartial, yellow sun peeked over the horizon and we sat in a café drinking coffee and taking strange glances from restaurant patrons who no doubt wondered who the hell the guys in cammies were—we laughed and shook our heads and did not tell one another that we had all been scared to death; to have been otherwise would have been the mark of a complete fool.

Yes . . . the little trail is fading from view . . . *I would not want to be here at night.*

Ahead of us approaches another island. This one looks to be about twice as big as the one already passed. I am guessing one hundred and fifty feet by seventy-five feet. We can see an old campsite peeking out from the enclave's perpetually dark floor. Again no one seems inclined to stop. Storm clouds, brewing like black mushrooms over the mountains of Mexico, have begun moving our way. Within minutes the first minor monsoon brushes over us, then moves eastward. We will have reached a widening in the channel, an area with no islands, when the next series of clouds catapults BB pellet raindrops into our midst. We huddle inside parkas and plastic covers, like turtles retracted into their shells, for twenty minutes before the sun finally reappears.

It will be on a subsequent trip, this time with only one canoe and two fellow adventurers (Larry Ditto and John Martin) that I at last gain entrance to the leaf-covered earth of the lost islands. This second trip is as purposeless as the first, which, of course, is the only type of trip worth taking—for only in a purposeless trip can one find purpose. Now we are free to think and feel, because no objective has occupied and thus distracted our minds.

Again, I am lost within a fresco of Huckleberry thoughts. I will live on this island alone, unencumbered by the policies and politics of the lands that surround me. I will not know the news, nor will I care. Because I will know privacy, and I alone will decide what my day looks like.

I sit beneath a granjeno grown twice as large as it would have were this same spot in the upland regions to the east and west. My *compañeros* are discussing something, but I can no longer hear them. I am already setting my Huckleberry trout lines and building my Huckleberry cabin. My Huckleberry stew and coffee await me. I peek out at a passing wooden dinghy, a local resident traversing his own superhighway, but I go unnoticed. I am incognito—a mass of tall trees and vines and cool earth.

The Good Earth Cabin

We lived in a cabin nestled in ninety acres of woods. It was the old place my grandfather had dubbed El Ponderosita, back in the days when the little ranchito had been surrounded by thousands of acres of *monte verde.* But in the years that had followed, the ranch had become nothing more than an island refuge: a green speck among miles of tilled desolation. Still, it was home, the place where I had learned much of what I know about the Brushlands; and inside this wooded confine where we lived from August, 1989, to October, 1992, Norma and I felt safe, well apart from that destructive madness that seems to possess so many.

If the cabin belonged to anyone, then it was Matthew's. It was our little boy's first true home. When Matthew was born, he and Norma moved to Norma's parent's house in Sebastian. We weren't happy with the arrangement, but like so many others caught in a world that has lost its focus, we were victims of the high cost of living. Norma had to work, and so did I. Neither one of us wanted anyone but kinfolk to look after the baby. So we had no choice but to endure a fourteen-month separation: Norma taught in Santa Rosa, and I stayed on as an environmental reporter in McAllen.

Finally, we saved enough to build a small home. We asked my Uncle Bill and Aunt Margaret Valverde if we could erect the cabin on their land. Twenty by twenty-four feet. Two bedrooms. A kitchen and living room. Two closets. A porch. Not much, but we were in heaven.

Sitting on the porch that first night—a rising half-moon tracing the twisting outlines of aged mesquites and ebonies against the cabin's walls, and a gang of coyotes singing in the distance—I recall telling

Norma, as she cradled our sleeping little boy in her arms: "We eat and sleep inside, but our real home is the woods."

Life had slowed. The change was as dramatic as the morning calls of a hundred birds—wrens, woodpeckers, pyrrhuloxias, doves, flycatchers, kingbirds, orioles—and as sudden as the emerging sun. The rhythm of life was as peaceful as the balmy breezes that swayed the stout branches of comas, anacahuitas, and brasils, and as quiet as the star-laden nights that pushed hushed clouds overhead.

One week later at midnight, beneath the whitish cast of a full moon probing delicately between windblown shadows, we awoke to a grunting sound. "Isn't that a javelina?" Norma asked, as we both peeked out of the window. Circling counterclockwise, grunting and snorting, rooting at the railroad ties we had placed beneath the porch and alongside the cabin to keep out critters, the little pig rounded our *casita* once, twice, three times. Every night, for four nights, it repeated the ritual.

Another week went by. Raccoons began to appear; their first tenuous steps on the front porch woke us. Through the merest opening in the curtain, we watched obscure figures prowling between the porch support posts and the wall. Smaller shapes scaled Matthew's rocking horse, though they never quite got the hang of riding it. Then the entire clan ambled across the front yard to the mesquite tree next to the brackish well—okay for bathing, but no good for drinking. There, the coons unraveled the tidbits we'd placed for them. Sometimes, when I felt mischievous, I'd hit the light switch. Adults and juveniles would freeze, each sheepishly eyeing the others as if asking, "Do things seem different to you?" Then, like children caught in the act, the raccoons would skip off the porch and disappear.

At sunrise I often took Matthew for walks to the front gate. At first he was reluctant, not wanting to be too far from Mama. But within a few days he became accustomed to the strange surroundings.

"This is mesquite, Matthew. That's tasajillo. This is coma. Over here we've got lote bush. Now don't step there, son. A coyote did that."

We had friends from town who came to visit us. But like many urbanites, they only wanted to shoot things—birds, rabbits, squirrels, lizards. One friend told us his son wouldn't come with him unless he could "kill something." Another long-time friend said he enjoyed shooting rabbits because that provided food for the coyotes, as if the coyotes had not gotten along just fine before he came along.

Perhaps this obsession to shoot animals for the sake of killing vents some pent-up aggression, a result of living in stress-filled cities. But for us, the rabbits, raccoons, javelinas, opossums, ground squirrels, bobcats, and coyotes that lived just beyond the edge of our yard were our neighbors, almost like part of our family. So when friends showed up with firearms, we told them they could keep their guns for protection but that we didn't abide killing critters.

Matthew was the one who first noticed the big male bobcat that claimed our picnic table as his personal bed and lookout perch. "What's that?" Matthew asked as we drove in one October (1989) night, after going to town to visit my parents.

The husky tom lay like an old hound—head plopped on his front legs, snout drooping over the edge of the table, his deep amber eyes reflecting the bright lights from the Land Cruiser. Stopping the Toyota to watch, I couldn't help feeling that we had crossed an intangible barrier. We were now just one more in a diverse family living in harmony within this small ecosystem.

"Let me see if I can walk up on him," I said.

Norma inched the truck behind me. I stepped closer and closer. When I was only about ten feet from him, the cat hopped off the table—no snarls or growls—and with a hip-swaying gait ambled disgustedly into the woods.

"If he comes back we'll just leave him alone," I said. About an hour later, he returned. Thereafter, the picnic table was his.

WINTER 1989–90

"We need a tree for Matthew's presents," Norma said one cloudy morning a few days before Christmas.

"But we don't want one of those pine tree jobs that people pay thirty bucks for—do we?" I asked.

"Of course not," she said. "Besides, it wouldn't look right out here."

So I found a long and straight guayacan branch, a solid mantle of dark green leaves obscuring the wood underneath, and put it in a rubber pot half-filled with soil. Norma placed our "tree" in Matthew's room, then she and Matthew wrapped a swirl of lights around it, hung a few ornaments on the branching stems, and began packing presents underneath. We took pictures on Christmas morning—a still, dark gray day with a windless chill in the air—and we sang Christmas carols and told Matthew the story of baby Jesus.

Only a few friends could relate to how we lived. Some of our relatives saw us as eccentrics. Strange how quiet, natural settings have become so foreign to most people: "How can you stay out here, all by yourselves, with the coyotes and snakes?"

SPRING AND SUMMER 1990

The mesquite trees were laden with leaves, yellow-green, the fresh patina of life renewed. Mourning doves, white-winged doves, white-tipped doves, ground doves, and Inca doves exchanged melancholy notes that sifted transparently through the woods. And in the late afternoons I went for my walk.

I have long felt that a day without a walk is a day lost and without purpose. Walking restores the spirit. I moved with the same timid curiosity of a child, following trails that led ambiguously into scores of options and fascinations, and places that had never been discovered in exactly the same way now presented. I roamed slowly; to do otherwise was to miss, and thus lose, the essence of the moment.

Most of the time there was no direction in those solitary treks. I merely filled my senses with every color and scent and sound available. I moved from stimulus to stimulus, following feelings instead of intellect. Time had no meaning, distance no relevance. I simply began to walk, allowing the spirit to guide me. Periodically, I stopped or sat, or simply rested on the warm ground looking up at the clouds, enjoying the symmetry of some old tree, listening to the calls of a bird, watching a beetle cross in front of me, inspecting a flower, touching a leaf, filtering the soil between my fingers, pinpointing the source of some enchanting fragrance, watching a ground squirrel scurry in and out of its burrow. There was never a routine; I was not out to build a better cardiovascular system or to race in a manic fury, like some people, from point A to point B. (Once in the Chisos Basin in Big Bend National Park, I overheard a conversation between two female park rangers. The first woman said, "This man just told me that he walked that six-hour trail in less than four hours. He was so proud of himself." The other ranger shook her head. "Gosh, you should have told him, 'What was the point?'")

When I roamed the woods, I invariably toted a rifle. But it was an old habit acquired many years ago when I walked with Papagrande. My habit is akin to that of one who never leaves the house without a pocket knife, which may hardly ever be used but is there just in case the need arises. I usually carried a battered Browning 92 in .357 caliber, or sometimes a sweet, little Brno .22 Hornet that I've owned for nearly thirty years. Neither rifle has been used for anything other than an occasional dirt clod or prickly pear pad in a very long time. I am still the hunter, but old woods roamers know what they can do; they do not need to prove themselves to anyone.

One late afternoon I entered a meadow about half an acre in size. As I walked between the licorice-scented hierba dulce plants, I noticed an elongate, sparkling black object lying on the ground in front of me. At first, I could not believe what I was seeing. There are no rocks in the area, and yet there before me was a perfect obsidian arrowhead, about two inches long, its edges as razor sharp as the day it had been made—perhaps a thousand years before. As far as I know, the nearest obsidian quarries are hundreds of miles to the south in Mexico. Was this arrowhead taken in trade, perhaps from some Indian who wandered far into Mexico, or was it brought to the area by the person who made it, on a hunt or a raiding expedition? Over the years I have found many arrowheads, bird points, and spear points at El Ponderosita, but that obsidian point was different. The question of its origin required some pondering—twenty minutes of serious daydreaming as I traveled a millennium into the past.

In early June we had a few days of intense rain. The wet ground gave me a good opportunity to take a census of the animals present on the property. In a pouch, I carried a field journal, two animal track guides, a magnifying glass, a measuring tape, a pair of binoculars, and a knife. When I found a set of tracks, I measured carefully the length and width of each footprint, the length and width of the stride, and any peculiarities about the stride or the prints, like foot deformities or the dragging of a paw. I found six different bobcat tracks—although one of those sets may have belonged to a large feral cat. I found ten tracks that I could positively identify as belonging to different coyotes.

I found a set of dog tracks, which belonged to a large dog owned by a neighbor who lived about a half-mile to the south. I found the tracks of five deer and three fawns. I discovered that there were three groups of javelina living, at least part of the time, on the place. The smallest javelina group contained six members, the largest eleven.

I identified the tracks of long-tailed weasels, raccoons, gray shrews, least shrews, badgers, gray foxes, striped skunks, and a spotted skunk. While I was taking the measurements of what were obviously skunk tracks, I looked up and saw an eastern spotted skunk watching me from about fifteen feet away. The breeze was blowing from me to the skunk so I had missed that valuable cue. The skunk did a handstand and fired, but the stream fell short by about four feet because an anacahuita shrub deflected it. Naturally, I got the hell out of there. I also identified the tracks of Mexican ground squirrels and the Mexican spiny pocket mouse and hispid pocket mouse, both of which mice I observed on numerous occasions.

But perhaps the most intriguing tracks belonged to a catlike animal that had a peculiar loping, or weasel-like, gait. The hind tracks measured exactly three centimeters in width and 41 millimeters in length. The right front paw measured 33 millimeters in width and 42 millimeters in length. The walking stride, from the front of the rear paw to the back of the front paw, averaged 69 centimeters. Being rather conservative by nature, I would have considered this track to be that of a small feral cat had I not seen the creature one afternoon. As I rounded the sendero on the far west edge of the ranchito, I noticed an animal that indeed looked like a large weasel (about ten pounds), with a vivid burnt sienna coat, crossing from east to west and about sixty yards away. I did not have time to use my binoculars, but the sighting remains well printed in my mind. The most distinctive characteristic of the animal's stride was the way it arched its back as it walked. I jogged quickly to the spot where it had crossed the sendero, but only two tracks were good enough to record. The following is what I wrote in my journal as I sat on the ground looking at the faint tracks:

> (June 12, 1990) These are the same tracks that I observed two days ago about a hundred yards west of the cabin. I desperately want to say that this is a jaguarundi—the thought that it might be has me so thrilled

> that I can barely contain myself. Nonetheless, I must remain cautious in my conclusions. If I had only been 25 yards closer, I'm sure I could have made a positive I.D. Will I ever get lucky again—lucky enough to spot this elusive creature crossing a sendero at close range? Or will I have to content myself with the tracks, and a brief glimpse (65 cm? plus 65 cm tail?)?

I never saw the creature again, nor did I record any more of its tracks. But if it was a jaguarundi, then that makes two that I have seen on the U.S. side of the Rio Grande.

FALL, WINTER, SPRING 1990–91

Since 1986, I had written a number of articles in the *McAllen Monitor* on the dangers of insecticides, herbicides, and defoliants. Most striking in the reaction when these articles appeared was the way that farmers defended the use of such poisons despite the overwhelming data that they are exceedingly dangerous. Of course, insecticides have saved lives and protected crops in many parts of the world, but their unrestrained application in the Rio Grande Valley, where over one-third of all the poisons doused on Texas soils are used, has created untold devastation both to the environment and to public health.

One afternoon I was sitting in the cabin listening to a radio talk show host compare automobile accident deaths with insecticide exposure deaths. The host said that one's chances of dying from an automobile accident were two thousand times greater than one's chances of dying from insecticides. Based on the radio host's remarks, I am sure some listeners concluded: *"If that's the case then insecticides must not be too dangerous."*

As I was learning, however, some people *want* to believe that pesticides do not pose a serious threat to our health or to the environment. Because these people are so eager to accept (or promote) false information, they are quick to buy into misleading statements. In fact, the same crowd often endorses similar rationalizations when the subjects of rampant deforestation or toxic dumping arise.

But the sophistry of comparing automobile deaths to pesticide deaths will not deter anyone who takes the time to study the facts. Yes, thousands die every year in automobile accidents. But what do we really know about insecticide (or herbicide, defoliant, and fungicide) illnesses? The statistic quoted by the talk show host compared only *immediate* deaths: people killed in car accidents versus people who ingested insecticides, or who somehow died after direct exposure to farm poisons. It did not consider the farmer who contracts lymph cancer after long-term contact with agricultural chemicals. Nor did it examine the etiological factors rooted in farm chemicals that predispose so many farmworkers to acquiring certain cancers and immunological disorders. Then there's the rural resident diagnosed with systemic lupus erythematosus because, over time, her immune system has been altered by low-dose chemical exposure. We must also speculate about the housewife diagnosed with breast cancer that might be traced to accumulation of agricultural poisons in her body. And don't forget the urban child who labors through chronic asthmatic attacks caused by farm chemical irritants wisping many miles through the air; and the thousands of people living in farming areas who yearly come down with strange maladies ranging from severe allergic rhinitis or flulike symptoms to sudden unexplainable bouts of "nerves" or "fatigue," also caused by farm chemicals. People whose sickness has been caused by agricultural chemical exposure do not get lumped into a ludicrous statistic comparing automobile deaths and insecticide deaths. Unfortunately, many doctors, who have not been trained to make the connection, venture only a tenuous assumption that so many illnesses found in farming areas *might* have had their genesis in agriculture chemicals.

But as an environmental reporter, I was learning that the chemical and agricultural industries exert tremendous pressure to stifle the truth. Profits rule. While conducting a telephone interview with a public affairs representative from a major agricultural chemical manufacturer, I was told that farm poisons "are as safe as mother's milk." That the man had the audacity to say what he did underscores the lengths to which chemical companies go to mislead the public.

But what about those who apply the chemicals? Might it be said that they too lack compassion for the consumer? So often throughout my stint as a journalist I witnessed the callous, perhaps even hyper-instrumental, demeanor of certain farmers. This was epitomized by farmers who *knew* they were poisoning the food they produced.

One day I was told that most farmers will not allow their own families to eat cucumbers. "We really nuke those cucumbers," a farmer said. He gave no thought to selling the "nuked" cucumbers to the general public. Yet wasn't this mentality the same as that of the street pusher who doesn't care about selling drugs to innocent kids?

The effects of chemical poisons on the public health and environment of South Texas are everywhere. One morning a photographer who worked at the *McAllen Monitor* told me that on the previous day he had been driving to an assignment near the town of Elsa. As he drove down a county road, a crop duster flew low overhead saturating a field with cotton defoliant. The photographer had his car windows rolled up, but that precaution did little good. Within seconds he was choking and wheezing. As he talked to me, he said he was suffering from dizzy spells, and that he had vomited twice the night before. He later developed a case of bronchitis and severe rhinitis.

About a month later, a man called me to say that he had watched a covey of bobwhite quail die after they were sprayed by a crop duster. Another man called to report that an acquaintance of his had gone temporarily blind after he was accidentally sprayed by a tractor that was spreading a powerful herbicide along the edge of a field. And a woman who lived west of Edinburg came to see me one afternoon because she had been reading my stories on farm poisons in the paper, and wanted to tell what had happened to her.

"You're the only person who I feel I can talk to," she said. "The Sheriff's Department doesn't care, the farmers don't care, the government doesn't care."

"What happened?" I asked.

Tears welled up in her eyes as she spoke. "I was sprayed by a tractor working a field that's next to my house. I suffered a horrible convulsion, and I developed a temporary paralysis that lasted for three days. Now I'm worried it might have done something that will make me sick in later life."

"You mean cancer," I said.

"Yes, maybe. I don't really know," she said. "It's just that I feel so alone. The farmers get away with murder. At least that's what I think. When I told the farmer what had happened, he just said that I should have gone inside and closed my windows. He made it sound like it was my fault."

"So what did you say to that?" I asked.

"I told him that he should have warned me that he was going to spray poisons. But he said he didn't have to because he wasn't spraying from an airplane."

"Airplane," I repeated—perhaps unconsciously.

"Can you believe it?" she asked. "The bastard said he didn't have the time to go around warning people when he was going to spray."

While working at the *McAllen Monitor* I began writing a column entitled "The Good Earth," the first column dedicated to environmental issues in deep South Texas. Until then, the environmental movement in the Rio Grande Valley had, for the most part, been an esoteric exercise conducted by a few dedicated individuals who were virtually unknown outside their own small circle. Which was exactly what some factions wanted. Those who abused the land looked at the Frontera Audubon Society, the Sierra Club, Bird Rescue, and the Wildlife Corridor Task Force as nothing more than a minor nuisance. But when "The Good Earth" came along, it provided dedicated conservationists like Benito Treviño, Jim and Cyndy Chapman, Dina Saldaña, Mary Lou Campbell, Joe Ideker, John Martin, and many others with a direct avenue to the general public.

The column and my investigative stories on brush destruction and on the dangers of agricultural chemicals infuriated the land abusers because until then, they had experienced no serious opposition. Now such subjects as poisonous agriculture, desertification, toxic dumping, sugarcane-field burning, water pollution, air pollution, and other related environmental issues were raised in public weekly.

Shortly after this column began appearing I received threats; I referred to them as my Bubba Phone Calls. Several times representatives of the Rio Grande Valley's farming community marched into the *McAllen Monitor*'s offices demanding that I be fired. On at least two occasions agricultural chemical company representatives issued statements that they were pulling their advertising from the paper. Yet, for every Bubba Phone Call I or my editor and publisher received, we took at least twenty calls from grateful readers who appreciated the truth.

One night after attending a meeting at the Texas A&M University

Extension Service in Weslaco, I was approached by a man who said he wanted to discuss my latest "Good Earth" offering. My Sunday column that week had been based on an article written by Dr. Bob Breene, an entomologist who worked at the Texas A&M Agricultural Experiment Station, also located in Weslaco. Breene had suggested using other methods of controlling insects besides the reckless application of poisons. He added that more research should be done on finding safe, biological checks like the use of beneficial insects. In my column, I alluded to the fact that farmers seemed wedded to their poisons. I also mentioned that a local radio station's noon farm program might be called "The Chemical Show" because it was one poison commercial after another. Though that particular statement was intended in jest, the immediate reaction from farmers and chemical interests showed just how desperate the local agriculture industry had become. The day after the column appeared, chemical representatives denounced it at a special meeting, and a group of farmers marched into the newspaper's offices threatening to do "whatever" to get me fired.

As I recall, the man who asked to talk to me that night in Weslaco was the local head of A&M's Extension Service. We went to his office, and for nearly an hour I was lectured on the wonders of farm chemicals. While I'll readily admit that insecticides have played a useful role in ridding the earth of certain diseases like malaria and yellow fever, I am adamant that herbicides and especially defoliants function chiefly to destroy the earth. Defoliants used on cotton crops in South Texas serve only one purpose: to make it easier for cotton picking machines to harvest cotton. But at what price? Arsenic acid, for example, leaches into the groundwater; other defoliants sweep through the air or contaminate the soil. The spectrum of horrors wrought by these dangerous chemicals convinces me (and many others) that their use near towns and settlements is nothing short of nefarious.

And yet, the man who had lectured to me for nearly an hour refused to listen to my point of view. I began to wonder whether he worked for Texas A&M or whether, in fact, he was employed by the chemical industry. He did not want to hear about the pathologies created by so many farm chemicals. He was not interested in the environmental mess brought on by defoliants, herbicides, insecticides. He dismissed all research indicating that farm chemicals did more harm than good.

In the end, he said: "Prove that farm chemicals cause all those illnesses you speak of."

To which I replied: "The burden of proof is not on me, but on *you.* Prove to me that farm chemicals are *not* dangerous."

I was accused of being anti-farmer. That was the easiest way out for those who did not like what I had to say. Far simpler to turn me into a villain than to address the facts. But the truth lay elsewhere. I was opposed to the unbridled destruction of the earth, period. It just so happened that farmers (and ranchers) had wreaked more havoc on the South Texas environment than any other group. Perhaps if I had lived farther west I might have spoken out against the clear-cutting of coniferous forests or against strip mining. But in my part of the world the instigators of destruction were those who manned the bulldozers and rootplows, those who flew the crop dusters or drove the tractors spraying megatons of poison, and those who allowed the soil to blow away by keeping the land barren.

If a man commits murder or peddles drugs then I am against that man. But I am not against *all* men. Likewise, I was not against all farmers. When I learned that a small group of brave men and women had broken with tradition and were implementing organic (nonchemical) farming methods, I was quick to publicize this. In my opinion the organic farmer is a hero standing alone—an island of reason in a polluted sea.

SUMMER AND FALL 1991

Life was evolving in two places. There was the world outside the woods: that manufactured place where men and women live fictitious lives wrapped within a veneer of vanity, symbols, and schedules. There was the world within the woods—unpretentious, without facades, still and quiet. As a reporter I was forced to venture into that outer world. But El Ponderosita, like Los Lobos Penninsula in Zapata County had been, was home.

There was another gift from Texas Heaven on the way. I remember the afternoon when Norma told me her home pregnancy test had come out positive. I think she was scared that I would be upset. And I can remember the look on her face when I hugged her and told her how much I loved her.

Magazine articles were now taking precedence over my newspaper work. I never questioned whether or not it was a bad time to leave the *McAllen Monitor.* In my heart I knew God would take care of us, as always. When I told Jack King, who had been the paper's captain since I had begun working for it in 1986, that I was leaving, he said he understood. He also said some nice things about my reporting and my writing. Coming from him, they meant a lot. Jack was never afraid of the news. He allowed ambitious reporters to go in search of good stories. He wasn't intimidated by talent. Jack was a reporter's editor. The *McAllen Monitor* was extremely lucky to have him on staff for some three decades. It will be a long time before they find somebody as good as Jack King was.

Mornings were for reading, afternoons for writing, evenings for woods roaming, nights for more reading or looking up at the stars. It is amazing how few things one needs when one has found harmony with nature. There were no neighbors to impress or keep up with. There were no social events to go to—and waste time chattering about unimportant issues and frivolous gossip.

My oldest son, Nomar Esteban, was off at college, and Jason, my second oldest, was in school in McAllen. On weekends Jason would come to visit. He was into basketball at the time. We set up a small court on an old patch of asphalt near the front gate, and on Saturdays and Sundays we'd go out to watch Jason shoot three-pointers and make jump shots.

One afternoon—one of those late summer days when feathery clouds streak westward like filaments clutching the sun—Jason and I decided to walk to the far west end of the little ranch. As always, we intended nothing more than to observe the plants, the birds, and if we were lucky an animal or two.

As we rounded a bend along the west sendero and began walking north, I heard a faint humming sound behind me. I turned.

"Jason, look."

"What's it doing?" Jason asked, as we both instinctively ducked to the ground to avoid being spotted by the small airplane that had appeared from nowhere and was now hugging a plowed field at perhaps no more than fifteen feet off the ground, heading in a sort of muffled glide toward the large house about a half-mile away.

Before I could answer, pale blue bundles began emerging from the plane. The bundles (we counted seven) struck the ground like heavy medicine balls, bouncing in low arcs, then rolling to clumsy stops.

"Stay down," I said.

"This is unreal, Dad. Must be dope, don't you think?"

A blue pickup truck dashed out from behind a patch of trees, and as the plane climbed at a forty-five-degree angle then banked a hard right toward Mexico, two men jumped from the blue pickup and tossed the bundles into the truck bed.

Jason and I inched backward into thicker brush, then made our way north, where we walked the fence line to the cabin. A few months earlier, Norma and Matthew had watched another plane skirt the power lines that ran from the main gate to the cabin and then land near the same large house where the men in the blue pickup truck headed.

After walking back to the cabin, Jason and I drove to a pay phone about four miles away so I could call my friend Andy Funk, who worked for U.S. Customs. The next day Andy and I reconnoitered the drop zone. In the plowed field, we could see plainly the shallow craters where each bundle had landed. We could make out the pickup tracks leading toward the large house. Three days later, Andy showed up at the cabin with a young fellow dressed in blue jeans and white shirt, and who identified himself as a member of the U.S. Army Special Forces.

"This is what we'd like to do," said the man, speaking with a heavy Brooklyn accent. "We'd like to drop a team off here."

I guess he caught the look on Norma's face because he added: "You'll never know they're here."

"What will they do?" I asked.

"They'll stay in the woods, keep a lookout on that big house," he said.

"If they see anything suspicious, then they'll call us to come in," Andy added.

I smiled. Norma knew what that meant. "This might get dangerous for us out here," she said.

"No it won't," the Special Forces fellow replied, trying to be as reassuring as possible but—with that sharp Brooklyn accent—falling just a wee bit short of convincing. "You'll never know they're out here," he repeated.

Norma looked at me, then back at the man in blue jeans and white shirt. "We'll know they're out here all right," she said.

I could tell the man did not grasp what she meant. Perhaps he'd read too much of his own press, or like a lot of city folks trained to behave like commandos and woodsmen, he simply couldn't fathom the idea that people who lived in the woods probably knew more about concealment and tracking and living off the land than he could ever hope to know.

"You might try to stay hidden," Norma said, "but my husband will smell you out, then cut your sign, then end up wanting to go out and stand surveillance with you."

"Well," I told the man. "At least you'll need water."

"We can bring the water to you, Arturo," Andy said. "Then you can go take it to the men." Andy turned to the guy from Brooklyn. "Really, you won't be able to hide from these people—believe me."

The soldier still looked unconvinced. And I could tell that his cockiness was not sitting well with Norma.

"Let us think about it," I said.

A week later, Andy showed up. Here was a guy from Kansas who looked more Texan than most—starched jeans and denim cowboy jacket, white western straw hat, spit-shine black boots, a Colt .45 auto strapped on a belt holster that rode high in order to hug the small of his waist. Andy must have figured that the Special Forces would not be landing at El Ponderosita, so he offered an alternative suggestion.

"Why don't you set these—" he opened the trunk of his car and pulled out an olive-drab box "—along the senderos, and maybe on that road that leads toward that big house. These are sensors. You can put the control panel in the cabin. When someone walks near them, or when a car drives by, the sensors will radio a signal back to the house. You can keep a log of the traffic around here."

Bad idea.

The old saying that sometimes you're better off being ignorant sure made sense after a while. Like kids glued to a video game, like couch potatoes welded to the television, like would-be entrepreneurs watching stock market reports flash across a wall, we were now slaves to the local traffic report, courtesy of that little black box that kept us abreast at all hours of what was moving from point X to point Y to point Z. And yet, could there possibly be so much clandestine activity within a half-mile of where we lived? Sensors don't lie. The black box said, *Yes.* Suddenly, we did not feel as isolated as we once had.

Still, I tried my best to ignore the goings-on at the big house that stuck out of the brush eight hundred yards away like the Addams Family mansion. I did not give up my walks. I began paying particular attention to a family of barn owls that had set up house in an old deer blind, rickety and long past its last coat of paint, on the property bordering the west side of El Ponderosita.

From inside the cubicle, where some hunter had sat ten feet off the ground and thrown down the beer cans that now circled the blind, fragmenting, I'd hear loud hissing sounds. I'd climb the termite-infested ladder and peek carefully inside the old wooden box. Like UFO aliens peering back at me—narrow, black eye slits inscribed within an oval of furry feathers—the young barn owls returned my gaze. Bobbing their heads up and down and hissing loudly, they'd squeeze into the corner, between piles of owl pellets and bird poop, collectively trying to make themselves as small as possible.

A few weeks later the owlets were flying. I'd purposely steer my late afternoon walks toward the old deer blind. It was best when I arrived just as the sun sank beyond the horizon. The young owls would swoop out of the blind to hover above me, those gigantic black eyes peering down from about twenty feet. Then the birds would perch in the tops of nearby mesquites to screech avian obscenities.

After a week of my sunset visits, the young owls became used to me. When they swooped out of the blind, they no longer screeched but instead, as if in suspended animation, levitated silently overhead. I'd raise my hand and say, "Be careful." Then I'd turn and stalk the sunset—a spirit in quest of eternity.

At the main gate, we were forced to enter the Other World: a place where people view the earth only in terms of its economic value. For Other World beings, the land is useless unless it can be exploited—turned into pasture, crop, or real estate. Beyond the main gate was a land so manipulated and tortured that it hardly looked real. The soil was plowed barren. The earth had been scraped clean, ripped open, turned, sterilized, and inoculated. It often smelled of pesticides and herbicides. When the winds blew, the Other World became like soup. Dust and sand whipped into turbulent storms, thick and choking.

I began talking more and more to the animals. They were not afraid, because I think they knew I meant no harm. I would tell them that I loved them—but not in some silly, Bambi way. I understood that they killed one another for food. And when my family needed meat, I would probably do the same. We knew the way of things. We accepted each other. We realized our fates. In that respect we were much alike. But the animals had had so much taken from them. I understood; so had I. We needed the same things. We shared the same enemies.

It seems to me now that while living at the cabin, I changed. Somewhere in that three-year journey, I shed the Man shroud, and adopted the Spirit dress. I came to terms with myself. Life beyond the woods no longer had meaning. Let people persist in their folly, play their political games, seek vain and shallow paths. *For me, there is only el monte.*

SPRING AND SUMMER 1992

Ethan arrived on December 6, 1991, the day after my forty-third birthday. Matthew, Jason, and I brought Norma and Ethan back to the cabin, then we all tried to pretend that El Ponderosita would not change further. Unfortunately, Other World Man would not leave us alone.

A land speculator cut a road through the middle of the ninety acres. True, there was a dedicated right-of-way bisecting the ranchito; we'd all known about it for years. But we had hoped this would never happen. Uncle Bill told the Other World Man he could have a key, so that he could use a trail established thirty years before. But Other World Man would have none of that. He brought his bulldozer and cut a fifty-foot-wide slash through the heart of El Ponderosita. Some of the thickest brush was shredded and leveled in less than six hours. Technology does great work when called on to destroy.

It would take a hundred years to replace what Other World Man had obliterated in half a day. He and his Other World friends looked on with pride at their accomplishment. But I remembered the ground squirrels, the javelina, the bobcats, the deer, the raccoons. And, of course, the big mesquites.

"These here trees should make damn good kindling," Other World Man said.

It was never quite the same after that. We'd hear cars traversing the new road at all hours. And then someone built a house and parked a small fleet of travel trailers at the end of the new road—wiping out a dense patch of chapote, comas, and anacahuita. We began hearing gunshots, even at night.

On one occasion we heard what sounded like a firefight coming from the big house a half-mile away. At around 2:00 A.M., we were awakened by the rat-tat-tat of 9mm submachine-gun fire, followed by seven quick shots from what I presumed was a .45 auto. At the same time, we heard about twenty evenly spaced (about a half-second apart) booms from what sounded like a .308 semiautomatic. About a minute went by, and then we heard more submachine-gun fire.

The next morning, I snuck up close to the big house, but it looked deserted. The raft of expensive cars and fancy pickup trucks that were usually parked outside were gone. Two dogs—a brown mutt and a overweight Rottweiler (the same beast that used to chase deer on El Ponderosita)—were the only signs of life. Using my binoculars, I scanned the parking area outside the house. Then I studied the house and the trees around it. I could see no signs of gun fire—no bullet holes, no broken glass. Then I swept the glasses farther south in the direction of a field from which, over the months, we had heard the sounds of planes landing and taking off. At the edge of the road that cut the field on the west side, I spotted something metallic shining in the morning sun. Then I saw other shining objects. I made a large semicircle, moving west, then south, then east, until I was directly across from the field, not more than thirty yards away. The sun had risen to about forty degrees above the horizon, and—like golden seeds sown along the edge of the field—I spotted hundreds of spent rounds.

What had been the scenario, I wondered? Had a plane landed and a rip-off been attempted? Had a meeting in the field gone bad?

There was no use calling the feds. Besides, Norma and I had decided that the narcs, with the exception of Andy Funk, were useless if asked to work beyond the city limits. A few months earlier, Andy had brought another U.S. Customs agent with him to look the land over. This fellow, about thirty years old, had no interest in the project. He didn't want to study tracks, nor did he even bother to look from side to side as we walked a trail. He was noisy, clumsy, and arrogant. He refused to follow directions—considering himself a hotshot agent.

"This is the kind of idiot who will get you killed," I told Andy as we moved off to check some sign, leaving Agent Hotshot back on the trail.

"It's getting too crazy out here," Norma said, as we discussed what I'd seen in the field next to the big house. I nodded, knowing that there was a subtle message in her remark.

In late July of 1992, while working on a magazine piece in Brownsville, I was bitten by some fleas. Ten days later I came down with a high fever, headache, extreme abdominal cramps, and malaise that knocked me to the ground. Three weeks passed before the diagnosis of typhus was made, and not until mid-September did my strength begin to return. Little did I know that the days of the Good Earth cabin were quickly coming to an end.

Norma began complaining of joint pains in early October. The pains and then stiffness progressed to the point where she could hardly move. We suspected arthritis, and as bad as that could be, we would gladly have lived with it instead of what we found out: she had systemic lupus erythematosus.

Perhaps the trauma of giving birth—coupled with a predisposition for lupus—had brought on the disease. We will never know. I strongly suspect that the pesticides and defoliants constantly sprayed throughout the Rio Grande Valley played a part in her developing the illness. There seems to be an inordinately high incidence of lupus in deep South Texas. Besides, as a young girl, Norma had worked in the fields in North Dakota and California, where she and her family had often been sprayed by crop dusters.

In December, 1992, we moved the Good Earth cabin off the ninety-acre ranchito to a lot I owned in Palmview, west of Mission. The little cabin looked lonely and out of place sitting in the middle of suburbia. I hoped it forgave me for moving it so far from the woods; it was just a house, of course, and houses have no feelings, but that little house was filled with memories. I hoped that the next family who lived in it would treat it kindly.

By the time we moved the cabin, we had already retreated to Norma's parents' home near Sebastian in Willacy County. After several months, thank God, Norma finally went into remission. Though her parents were extremely kind to us, Willacy County proved an ordeal. The area is one plowed field after another. Crop dusters shed poisons across the landscape like mongrel dogs dropping ticks across one's yard. Every day, we'd hear the airplanes, and the stench of sundry insecticides, herbicides, and defoliants blew systematically over the ground. We were glad when we finally left the county to seek quieter and cleaner places far away.

On the day that the Good Earth cabin was moved, Norma, Matthew, and I were there to videotape the event. It was sad, but I kept my composure. There were so many recollections, after all. For thirty-seven months the little house had served as our home. I looked down the sendero that led west by southwest from the cabin, and I remembered my afternoon walks. I glanced at the picnic table and thought about the bobcat that slept atop it. I saw a rabbit skip into the brush, and I hoped that no one would know it was there.

Norma watched through the video camera lens as the truck carrying the cabin inched its way along the road leading east from El Ponderosita. When the truck and cabin were about a quarter of a mile away, she pushed the fade button.

"We'll have to find another patch of brush," I told her.

She smiled, kissed me, then said, "Don't worry, we will."

.44 Henry

The spent .44 Henry cartridge was lying on the road I'd walked a thousand times. It was off to one side, near an outcropping of bristly tasajillo cactus, half submerged in the hard-packed, sandy-clay soil, its tarnished rim neatly indented by the pale thrusts of twin firing pins. I wondered how many years it had been there. And in the same thought, I imagined the times when others had roamed the brush as I now did.

Suddenly, from beyond the long shadows of a rising sun, a man appeared. He was standing between two large mesquites: trees that had endured a century of immense change. Atop his head he wore a broad-brimmed felt hat, sweat stained and tattered. He had loose-fitting tan canvas trousers and a frayed, long-sleeved brown cotton shirt. His boots were knee-high and scuffed, the black they had once been now faded into patches of eroding gray. On his waist was an inch-wide leather belt holding a deer antler–handled knife and a small white cloth pouch. In his hand he carried a long, octagon-barreled lever action rifle, its solid brass receiver dulled from use.

He was looking straight ahead and hadn't noticed me, half hidden behind a sprawling nopal cactus. I turned to see what he was eyeing, and I spied a young white-tailed buck, his antlers barely visible above a large purple sage bush.

The man moved cautiously, sidestepping fallen twigs and decaying leaves. Then he stopped, his hat barely brushing a low-hanging thorny branch. Slowly, eyes fixed, head rigid, he brought the rifle's hammer to full cock.

The buck had not spotted the man who stood between him and the climbing sun; a gentle northerly breeze was sweeping through, wicking the hunter's scent away. The man inched closer, his route bringing him to within ten feet of where I stood. Then abruptly, he stopped. And for a long breath his eyes met mine, though neither one of us said a word.

Finally, he turned and carefully raised his rifle. For an instant time dissolved into a deciduous haze, and I did not hear the gun's crack, nor did I see the man walk away. I presume the buck fell, but later on I could locate no traces of blood. Instead, all I found was the .44 Henry case the man had left behind.

El Venado

In all the years of hunting white-tailed deer—of waiting along senderos, or propped in uncomfortable positions in old mesquite trees, and then catching colds or 'flu from overexposure—I don't think I've learned anything other than that *el venado grande* will do exactly what you don't suppose at the instant you least expect it.

One December morning back in 1971 I "called" in a skinny eight-point buck during a coughing fit. In June of that year I had had a tonsillectomy, and though six months had passed, I had yet to recover fully. Occasionally, when I swallowed, I'd have to cough.

That morning as I walked along a sendero, I felt my throat growing tight. The coughing fit lasted about thirty seconds, and when I looked up, I saw the buck blazing a trail right at me. I shall not forget the surprised look in his eyes when he spotted me and realized that the coughing was not the snorting of a lovesick doe.

Then there was that time in 1976 when I was walking back to camp after a long afternoon spent wedged into the fork of a grizzled old mesquite. I remember that I was transfixed by the silhouette of a great-horned owl perched atop an ebony tree that stood directly in front of a setting, carmine sun.

Spotting movement to one side, I stopped and waited. From behind a thorny brasil tree walked a ten-point buck, his head held low to the ground, his stride labored—as if he had been running for many miles. He passed within thirty feet of me, seemingly without a clue as to my presence, then lay down beneath the ebony tree where the owl was. I sat slowly and watched. The buck's coat looked silver-gray, an effect created by dark gray hairs tipped by specks of white. Perhaps he was just old. Presently, he put his head down, leaning his wide antlers on the side of the ebony, and went to sleep. I had not the heart to disturb his dreams. So after what seemed to be a long wait, though it probably wasn't more than a few minutes, I stood and tiptoed away.

While hunting on a lease west of San Isidro, I shot what I have since referred to as my "sandwich" buck. As is typical during South Texas winters, that day in late December of 1983 was hot and dry. Since dawn I'd sat between two granjeno shrubs, watching a trail and game crossing. Three does, a coyote, and a squatty badger had emerged at the crossing, but no buck had appeared.

At noon I decided to walk back to my truck for a sandwich and a glass of water. I placed a folding stool along a narrow *brecha* about thirty paces from my truck, opened my lunchbox, and dug into a peanut butter sandwich I'd prepared. I had barely gotten halfway through the meal when I spotted two bucks—a fat eight-pointer and a long-legged six-pointer—crossing the brecha about sixty yards away. Quickly I grabbed my rifle and, still chewing, began to stalk the larger of the two animals. It was a short little hunt, though even this was not as brief as another a few years before.

I had been on my way to a deer stand made from cut mesquite branches placed against a corner fence post. When still about fifty feet from the stand, I noticed a quick movement: a frisky eight-pointer with two additional long drop tines was staring at me from behind a coma tree. Usually, a successful hunt concludes after hours of being on a stand or following a long stalk. But this time I had just arrived, and I had missed sunrise by at least two hours. Not about to let the opportunity slip by, I placed a well-aimed .280 Remington bullet from a custom Ruger single shot into the buck's neck.

For me, the best hunts have always come when the shots are close. I am not one for sitting in tall towers, sealed away from the elements. In 1967, I took an eight-pointer that I believe defines what whitetail hunting should be. The morning was cold and misty, the dampness having given the ground the soft texture of fine carpet. The eight-pointer was not a "trophy" in the conventional sense, but perhaps established criteria for judging the quality of a remembrance should be based less on antler size and more on the skill of both hunter and prey.

The buck—his gray, winter coat appearing almost black in the dark overcast—was feeding along a fence line about two hundred yards away. It would have been simple enough to have ended the chase there. Magnums and scopes turn such distances into routine work. But to me that seems unfair—for both prey and hunter. Relying on a high-powered rifle and scope to reach out and take an animal is really nothing more than putting technology to work; it says little about a hunter's worth in terms of skill or determination.

A shot at two hundred yards, as far as I'm concerned, would have diminished the hunt seriously. So I chose to get as close as I could. To my left, a group of about ten or twelve cows grazed placidly. Using them as cover, I circled and closed the distance between myself and the dark buck. In less than twenty minutes, I'd arrived at the spot where he had stood, but he was gone. Then I noticed that he had moved away from the fence and was now browsing about six *feet* away. I raised my rifle, but at that distance the four-power scope was much too powerful. It was a point-and-shoot proposition.

Naturally, when one decides that sitting in blinds and taking long shots is not the proper way to hunt whitetails, one must be prepared for failures. I think many hunters would opt for stalking and adopting better woodsmanship skills were it not for the fact that hunting has become so expensive; and most people just don't have the time to develop those kinds of talents. Let's face it, someone who can only spare a week or two out of the year to be in the woods will never become adept at reading sign or stalking.

In my younger days, I hunted at every opportunity. I have had the chance to shoot bucks with many different kinds of rifles. In all, I've found that most guns are too powerful for deer, if you have any intention of preserving the meat. Even the little .243 Winchester can be destructive if the shot hits the shoulder. Anything from a .270 up is simply too much for white-tailed deer, and why people insist on using those big cartridges speaks more for attitude than anything else.

In recent years, I've taken to watching animals more than shooting them. As my wildlife photographer friend Steve Bentsen puts it: "Most hunters sort of mellow out after the age of forty. They'd rather let the young hunters take the bucks." Besides, the old-timers, the ones who have hunted honestly and fairly, know what they can do.

The other reason I don't hunt much any more is because I don't like what passes these days for hunting in the Lone Star State. I see ranchers charging astronomical fees that few people can afford to pay. These same ranchers usually drive their "clients" around in pickups and four-wheel-drive vehicles until an "appropriate" buck is spotted. Sometimes, the dude hunter doesn't even leave the comfort of the truck but merely pokes the gun barrel out of the window, lines up on the deer, and calls it a hunt.

Not long ago, I was offered a tour of a deer blind on a ranch north of the town of Edinburg. The impressive structure had been built for a Houston businessman who had bought several thousand acres for deer hunting. Fifteen feet high and measuring six feet square, the blind was replete with television set, a small bed, a toaster oven, port-a-potty, refrigerator, and heater. Our dude hunter sits in the middle of the blind on a rotating bench that he merely pedals in order to swirl around and look through three large portholes. His rifle (I was told that it was a special job built expressly for making long shots down senderos) rests in a viselike apparatus. Our dude has also had range markers installed at fifty-yard intervals on the three senderos that converge at his blind. If, perchance, he should get bored sitting in all that luxury, he can climb out of his little house and into a customized truck that has special swivel chairs installed over the headlights for driving down quail, and which has a built-in retracting deer stand that telescopes to about ten feet over the rig.

I wonder what would happen if Texas suddenly outlawed the use of deer blinds, and prohibited everything other than replica black powder rifles like those used in the last century or recurve and long bows? The first group to cry foul would doubtless be the manufacturers who profit from this yearly long-range killing binge. Everybody who has contributed to making hunting less than what it should be would yell the loudest. Next would come all those dudes who have not the foggiest idea what a real outdoor experience is all about. Take away their fancy deer blinds, their hot magnum rifles with high-magnification scopes, make them walk and stalk, and they would all fall to the ground hysterical.

It seems that people have lost sight of the fact that real hunting pits hunter against beast on more nearly even terms. The human brain will always give us an edge, but we should strive to keep that edge within reasonable limits—if for nothing else, for a sense of honor. Every time we widen our advantage, whether by employing rifles that can shoot farther or by adding pulleys to archery gear, we belittle the honest experience of hunting.

For too many people, hunting has become nothing more than a status thing, placing hunter against hunter. Animals have become mere commodities caught up in human vanity.

Not long ago I saw a television program about deer hunting. In it were two well-known outdoor writers: men who have hunted worldwide and are considered great outdoorsmen. When they spotted a big mule deer, one man said: "Look at that! Gosh that's at least a 178." I guess those men could no longer look at a breathtaking mule deer buck and think of him as anything other than a number. The hunt, for them, was reduced to a contest—a way to show off.

In other places, the story grows sicker. A man I know who guides hunters into Mexico brags that he has the locals shoot bottle rockets into the air over duck ponds so that the ducks will constantly be flying back to the pond where his dude hunters lie waiting. "In about an hour," he says, "it's all over."

Still, there are those men and women—whom I admire greatly—who have refused to compromise the hunt, who insist on fair chase, who are masters at the long bow, who use primitive black powder rifles, or who, if they do employ modern firearms, never take a shot at over fifty yards. These are real hunters. And for them I will relate one more wild story about el venado grande.

A few years back on New Year's Eve, my son Jason met me at the ranch gate with a broad grin on his face. As he swung the gate open he called out, "I shot a buck."

Jason had been playing basketball, practicing jump shots and three-pointers when he spied a muscular twelve-point buck—nostrils flared, hoofs kicking the ground—at the edge of our makeshift court. The buck must have heard the ball being dribbled and presumed it was a fight in progress. Jason was spooked at first, but within seconds he had the presence of mind to drop the basketball and pick up a rifle he'd placed atop a picnic table. It took only one shot, and we had venison for the rest of the winter.

Los Lobos Revisited

We came to trace the same route that had led us to Los Lobos Peninsula back in 1986. With only five miles to go, we turned west off U.S. Highway 83 midway between the towns of Roma and Zapata—filled with faith, and anticipating the tranquility of Falcon Lake and the quiet woods surrounding it.

But this time, in July, 1995, a relentless, laser sun pulsated from above, and the earth broiled beneath an unquenchable dryness from many months without rain. I glanced in the rearview mirror still believing that, somehow, nine years had failed to make any sort of mark on that wonderland lying just down the road.

"This is where your mama and I used to live," I said.

In the back seat, two little heads with mushroom haircuts and big brown eyes took notice of the remark and intensified their assessment of the area.

But as we crossed the first cattle guard, we began to sense that all was not right. The lush fusion of greens that once inched their way out of the lake, as if furrowing gradually inland from the water, had vanished. Now, an acidic and treeless brown fanned out in nearly every direction.

"Let's go home," I said. But Norma remained quiet.

Everything had been bulldozed. At least ten thousand acres of brushland. *Gone.* For as far as we could see a scalding earth lay devoid of life. And Falcon Lake, too, had withered into a silty pond. From its stagnant, murky water jutted countless anorexic sticks of chalky-white mesquite—the remnants of mighty trees drowned decades ago.

What will happen when it does finally rain? I shuddered as that dark thought inched out from my subconscious. Black clouds would ooze westward from the Gulf of Mexico, or perhaps an arm from one of the scores of thunderheads that swell above the Sierra Picachos sixty miles to the west would extend eastward. The rains would begin suddenly, as they always do in this part of the world. Lightning would hammer the barren hilltops; thunder would quake through the ravines. The gray deluge would mop its way from one end of the landscape to the other—the soil bubbling in the pelting rain, then sweeping through gorges: a chocolate mixture of dirt, sand, and water hurdling rocks and decaying tree trunks, then finally flushing into the lake.

Days later, when the sun returned in force and the southeast breezes once again brushed velvet shadows beneath lofty clouds, the earth would be still and vacant. A few broken sticks would lie half submerged in the cracked and hard mud. Only the termites would find food in so many piles of bulldozed brush, now scattered by the rains that had come and gone.

"How could they have done this?" I asked aloud.

"I don't know," Norma said, barely above a whisper.

"Gosh, I feel so bad bringing our children to this. And then to tell them that it was once so beautiful."

Norma did not reply. She had obviously decided that talk had become inappropriate. She knew there was nothing she could say.

We rounded the last curve that descended for nearly a mile and ended at Los Lobos Trailer Park. What we saw seemed almost too hard to believe. Our walking trails that had meandered among the shady trees and gentle slopes had been replaced by refineries; the tall cracking chambers leaping out of the ground like malignant warts. And not only had the brush on our left and right been stripped away for as far as we could see, but the oil company that now possessed the land stretching to the southwest until it reached Falcon State Park had gashed an even deeper wound spanning at least one hundred feet in width and running for many miles. *Just so that they could lay a six-inch pipe.*

Along the pipeline, the oil company had placed more cancerous projections, which, ironically, they refer to as "Christmas trees." From these deformed contraptions of pipes and valves the oil people gauge the effectiveness of their god. One can only wonder about those who see the desecration of nature as productive.

"Well, hell," I hear them say. *"You drove your damn car out there, didn't you?"*

Yes, that's true. But does a six-inch pipeline require a scar a hundred feet wide that extends for miles? And does a solitary and very much cherished state park have to be raped? And who was it that convinced the local landowners to denude their land of its brush? And then *why* did they do it?

Some of us had asked those same questions two years before when we testified at the hearings held at Falcon State Park to determine whether or not more drilling was to take place there. Of course, they weren't really hearings because the decision had already been made. Still, we tried, because Falcon State Park was a tiny icon of what all the lands in the northwest corner of Starr County looked like before the bulldozer and rootplow—and the oil well—arrived.

At the hearings, Zapata County conservationist Dina Saldaña said: "We're wasting our time here, folks. This is a done deal." The representatives of the Bureau of Land Management smiled; the lone panel member from the Texas Parks and Wildlife Department fidgeted *(wasn't the park supposed to be under their stewardship?)*; the gelatinous mass of oil men and women, who outnumbered us ten to one, laughed.

Those of us who spoke in favor of nature did not call the oil people sociopaths, or earth rapers, or greedy slobs, or anything that might be construed as offensive. Though perhaps on reflection we might as well have called them those names. Because they called us tree huggers, butterfly chasers, environmental whackos, weirdos, and eco-nerds.

The last person to testify on behalf of the oil company was the Zapata County judge. "I don't give a damn about the trees!" the judge blared. "I care about my people. I care about the men, women and children of this county." The county judge looked directly at me and said: "You, Longoria. I know about your writings. You're just a damn tree hugger. But I care about people."

Dina Saldaña, standing in the back of the room, called out, "The only person you care about is yourself."

His voice high-pitched and angry, the county judge told Dina to shut up. "I want jobs for my people," the judge shouted. "To hell with the brush."

Benito Treviño got up to speak, but we could all tell it was over. The BLM people weren't even paying attention any more; the lone Texas Parks and Wildlife Department representative looked scared or embarrassed, or both; the oil people were already congratulating themselves; the Zapata County judge was in the corner talking to a journalist and pointing at a few of us in the audience.

A few months later that same Zapata County judge was sentenced to prison in a narcotics case. I guess the argument can be made that he cared about his people enough to get them hooked on drugs. Strange world, indeed.

And what of Falcon State Park? The oil wells went in. The brush was cleared. The starry nights disappeared somewhere beyond thousands of oil derrick lights. The quiet was smothered behind moaning pumps, grinding gears, rumbling diesels, clanking wrenches, honking horns.

"They've destroyed everything," I told Norma as we arrived at the town site of Old Falcon. We stayed only a few minutes.

We headed farther north, until we found another road leading to the lake. All the while I kept remembering how it used to be: The green woods, the sculptured clouds, coyotes singing in the distance, the ospreys and pelicans, painted buntings and prothonotary warblers, the cactus flowers, the solitary beaver at the water's edge, the star-laden nights.

Finally, we found a place that had not been visited by bulldozers, rootplows, and oil people—though I am sure they had looked the area over because oil company survey sticks lined the road.

"I need to walk," I told Norma and the boys.

"I understand," she said. "Matthew, Ethan and I will stay here by the truck and look at the flowers."

Here, the monte was not nearly as tall as it had been at Los Lobos Peninsula, but it was woods nevertheless. The cenizo was blooming, as was the whitebrush, the rattlebrush, and the *hierba del venado.* I knew it was only a facade, but I pretended that I was far away, and that sociopaths and earth rapers would never come here. I tried to forget what I had seen back at Los Lobos. I wanted to remember how it used to be. Then I looked down and saw that nature, despite the ravages of man, still struggled to overcome. There on the pebbled earth beneath me, I spotted an uncommon plant called *Croton ciliatoglandulifer.* I pulled my magnifying glass from my pocket and marveled at the delicate leaves, lined with tiny glands that looked as if the plant were once a star now come to rest in this isolated place.

In Texas *C. ciliatoglandulifer* has been reported to occur on small plots southeast of Roma in Starr County, and a few patches are found near the lower Gulf Coast. But no one, to my knowledge, had ever reported it so close to the town of Zapata. That it had survived the human butchery of the surroundings—that it holds a tenuous grasp on that rocky hill—seems amazing. But that is because we have learned to ignore the stench of exploitation. We have become accustomed to pretending that all is well, that isolated patches of brush are good enough, that massive scars really aren't that bad.

Making the Loop

I remember a summer afternoon back in the mid-1960s when I was sitting with Papagrande under the tin-roofed porch that stood next to the little brick cabin at El Ponderosita. My grandfather and I were talking about the woods, as we often did, our conversation backdropped by the serene coo of a lone mourning dove and the constant purring of hundreds of cicadas.

As if he had suddenly remembered something—a recollection that, perhaps, reached far back into his memory—my grandfather looked off at the high, cottony-white clouds wafting westward above us and said, *"Que linda vida."*

I nodded, and replied, "Yes it is, Papagrande."

If it was windy that day, I cannot recall. Besides, the stalwart defense of nearly impenetrable brush filtered out gusts and sand that might have had their origins in places far away. Humankind and its machines, and its interminable greed, faded into distant worries that could neither ford nor burrow through the mottled greens and browns that sprawled outward in all directions, immersing us in a tempered leisure. It was a good time to be alive; it was a good place to live.

Papagrande, though never formally educated, was a consummate ethnobotanist and naturalist. Of course, he didn't know the scientific names of the plants and animals, but he was nonetheless the kind of man people sought out when they wanted to learn the medicinal uses of a particular plant or the behaviors of some creature. He read animal signs as clearly as a learned man might read a scholarly book. He lived off the land with never a thought for want, for he abided in harmony with nature.

In those distant days, we could not have known that it would all disappear: that in twenty years, 96 percent of all the upland brush in deep South Texas would be bulldozed and rootplowed into oblivion. I'm glad that Papagrande did not live to see it all happen; though I know that before he died in 1973, he knew what lay on the horizon.

In 1969, as I have noted earlier, a wealthy McAllen businessman purchased the large tract of land that bordered El Ponderosita. He took advantage of the government program that paid landowners to clear the brush, and he turned some of Hidalgo County's finest *ramadero* woodlands into table-flat dirt in less than a week.

Neither Papagrande nor I said much about it. After all, what could we do? We'd stand at the edge of the ranchito and look north, remembering the tall mesquites and ebonies, the lush understory of cenizo, nopal, granjeno, anacauita, coma, brasil, tasajillo, coyotillo, salvia, crucillo, palo verde, ocote, chaparro prieto, amargoso, mejorana, junco, and scores of other small trees and shrubs that weren't there any more.

All gone . . .

And then we'd walk quietly back to the brick cabin, where we'd sit for a long time without saying a word. Yes, Papagrande knew what was coming. Maybe that's one reason he finally gave up and left, one summer's night in 1973.

It fell to me to stay and watch it all disappear. Now in 1996, only a scattering of the once lush deep South Texas Brushlands remain. Never mind that when the winds blow the skies became a khaki brown choked with sand and topsoil. Forget that the land—where deer, javelina, bobcats, badgers, raccoons, coyotes, jaguarundis, ocelots, ground squirrels, rabbits, tortoises, lizards, snakes, and birds roamed and crawled and nested—has been reduced to so much naked earth. The landowners, it would seem, are satisfied; their consciences are clean; their coffers are full. It has always been a matter of money, anyway.

Now at the end of the twentieth century, few people in deep South Texas feel any strong connection to nature, because for the most part it remains inaccessible. Those removed from the wilds have little chance of acquiring an allegiance to that world outside the city. Often, their only exposure to it has been delivered with the special sensory deprivation of television, where nature is reduced to another picture in the tube, void of real emotions, without smell, neither warm nor cold, and lacking entirely that quintessential somatic and emotional touch that only the real thing can provide.

Unfortunately, people who harbor no deep alliance to nature feel no compunction to save it. Nor are they likely to acquire a profound understanding of its complexity. With no genuine access to the outdoors, any primordial *need* to be one with the land, or to comprehend the multifold variations of its flora and fauna, is reduced to the artificial bliss of so many theme parks, zoos, city plazas; and now, to what must be considered the ultimate slander, "virtual reality." But in the process, a clear problem has been created: *If the common men and women of South Texas are unable to build a subjective union with the Brushlands, then those same people will see no reason to protect it.* Therefore, a process must be developed that will help the people of the region foster an emotional connection with the diverse habitats that once surrounded them but now are on the brink of extinction.

Ironically, those among us who desire to conquer the environment might eventually produce the opposite effect. We have witnessed in the last century an intrinsic process of de-evolution. Through habitat degradation and the uncurbed pollution of the biosphere, we have created a world that we will be hard pressed to evolve past. The adaptive urgency created by a desecrated earth makes no accommodations for the snail's-pace regimen of natural selection. But it was not always so. As hunters and gatherers, we were as much a part of the land as was any creature that existed on earth. This closeness to nature spawned cultural codes of conduct that created a reverence for living and nonliving things alike. We had to live acutely aware of how the land provided sustenance and security. Not until much later—when humanity adopted the sedentary lifestyle associated with large-scale agriculture—did land ethics begin to change. What had been essentially an ethos accepting our position in nature as one more part of a vast plant and animal consortium digressed into beliefs that placed the biotic and abiotic environment as subject to human whims and desires. Eventually, this anthropocentric outlook led to intense population growth and indiscriminate exploitation of the earth.[2]

The Lower Rio Grande Valley of Texas stands as one of the most denatured areas in the United States. According to the U.S. Fish and Wildlife Service, of the more than four million acres of brush that blanketed the landscape of the lower valley seventy years ago, less than 4 percent remains; and of the habitat that survives, about 50 percent grows on small tracts less than seventy-five acres in size.

Most of the desperate 4 percent of terrain still representative of the varied original habitats in the lower valley lies beyond reach of ordinary citizens. Whether part of the U.S. Fish and Wildlife Service's corridor stretching along the Rio Grande from Brownsville to Falcon Dam or scattered within the large ranches bordering to the north, the brush remains unknown for the majority of common people. Not that the animals and plants do not deserve a place of their own, as in the case of the Corridor. But any thought that protected habitats in the area will last into perpetuity seems frivolous, because generations of citizens who are unexposed to nature, or who have lost their primitive knowledge of how the land can provide nourishment for body and spirit, will develop no reverence for that which they have been denied.

There are essentially two ways of addressing the subject of environmental awareness and appreciation. The first avenue examines environmental *issues* and then seeks ways to address those issues. This method has been the primary means adopted by traditional educators. The typical scenario—which I call a technological approach because it presumes an answer to the problem of building a subjective union between people and nature without first asking, "What will really work?"—frequently suggests developing a workbook or film presenting the pros and cons of various environmental issues.[3] Notwithstanding the benefits of issue knowledge, that information alone does not promote the sort of emotional bonding with nature that can cultivate a profound desire to preserve the biosphere. Consider, after all, that spokespersons, lawyers, and executives for polluting companies are generally well versed on environmental issues, but they do not as a rule harbor acute desires to stop polluting or destroying the environment.

I have tested this hypothesis at the college where I now teach. By using interviews, questionnaires, and opinionnaires regarding environmental issue knowledge, and by exposing students to a litany of environmental workbooks, I have learned that most students have prior knowledge about these issues, gained mostly through television programs and documentaries but also from magazine and newspaper articles. As I had suspected, however, the vast majority of students express no predisposition to change their behaviors and adopt more biocentric lifestyles on the basis of having seen television programs or studied a workbook.[4] As one student noted during an interview: "Why can't we just build a great big vacuum cleaner that will suck in all the polluted air, and then clean it out—or why can't we build a dam in the Rio Grande that will act as a huge filtration system?" Television programs and environmental workbooks can inform students about issues; they can communicate facts, clarify arguments pro and con, but they *do not* instill any sense of what Aldo Leopold called, "a refined taste in natural objects," or what Dave Foreman calls, "an enthusiastic embracing of the philosophy of Deep Ecology and biocentrism."[5] As the views of the student quoted show, non-connected-to-nature individuals frequently opt for a recourse or remedy that relies purely on technology, or what

Daniel Chiras labels "Band-Aid measures."[6] People, therefore, need much more than mere issue knowledge if we are to expect them to give up their polluting lifestyles in order to save nature.

But if issue knowledge alone does not foster profound pro-nature attitudes, then what does? I am perplexed by those who insist that all things in this world should accommodate the "needs of man." That pervasive feeling has stretched across all levels of the social strata. What biologically selective good, one must wonder, can unrelinquished greed play on the endurance of humankind? Will this greed work, in the end, as some sort of negative feedback mechanism? Or perhaps we see (in the midst of uninhibited anthropocentric avarice) the first faint signs of an adaptive reversal—a sort of "founder effect" manifested phenotypically by the behaviors of those who express a sincere love for the earth and all that resides within and upon it.[7]

As I write this, I think back to just yesterday, when I and a group of students took part in a reforestation project south of the city of Donna. It was hard work, accomplished on a hot and cloudless day. But as we dug holes, placing the seedlings within those cool pockets of moist earth, and then covered the edges with dirt, I heard one of the students comment: "If anybody ever comes along and bulldozes this land, I'll kill 'em!"

How interesting, I thought. We can teach these students about the importance of biological diversity, we can lecture to them about the harmful effects of pollution and desertification, we can force them to study various biological topics from cellular respiration and photosynthesis to Mendelian genetics, and yet with all our academic prowess, we—the writers and teachers—get scarcely an angstrom of beneficial results by comparison with the effect of the simple act of asking a student to plant a tree. There is a linkage, it seems, between productively participating in nature and wanting to preserve it.

I should emphasize the word *productive* because there are many negative actions that can be taken in the outdoors. For example, root-plowing, bulldozing, mining, drilling, spraying poisons; in essence, anything that destroys habitat or lessens the diversity of life is a negative experience, which does not enhance that passionate love for the woods. Hunting and fishing, paradoxical as it may sound, are two of the best ways to introduce people to nature—especially if primitive hunting implements are used.

We do not need more textbooks or films on nature; we need more nature. I am amazed at all the conservation and preservation groups who want people to connect with the Brushlands, forests, and deserts, and who purchase large tracts of habitat, and who become so befuddled when people still do not seem to care about the *monte verde.* These same groups often insist on locking people out from the land. Why then should they wonder when people have no regard for saving habitats?

But glory be, let me clarify that remark before some slick-talking promoter walks up and says: "Yep, that's why we've got to open up the wilderness to motorcycles and RVs."

I am talking here about Texas—South Texas in particular. Most Texans don't enjoy the privilege of having access to millions of acres of public lands, as do the people in the American West. In Texas, the barbed wire fence and No Trespassing sign rule. Most Texans have no idea what constitutes wilderness; the average Texan's exposure to nature is a state park crisscrossed with asphalt roads and studded with picnic tables and RV hookups. Some Texans travel to Big Bend National Park believing that they've found wilderness. But nothing could be farther from the truth. The feds have placed a village—replete with Park Service subdivision, *turista* motel and restaurant, and ranger station—smack-dab in the middle of the most beautiful spot in the park: the Chisos Basin. Big Bend National Park is just what its name implies: a great big park, not wilderness.

Texans can travel to New Mexico, Colorado, Wyoming, Utah, and points farther north (though sometimes we are not entirely welcome) to enjoy wilderness. There places exist that do not allow motorcycles, RVs, snowmobiles, or anything else that spits out carbon monoxide and makes obnoxious noises. The "founder effect mind" needs places like that.

But in Texas, finding that kind of locale, as things stand now, is nearly impossible. Yet the more we lose control of our personal lives, and are unable to find any sense of real privacy, and are pummeled with an information overload, the more we are going to see these "founder effect individuals" coming forward and demanding wilderness. When I see certain politicians proclaiming that the West's public lands be turned over to their friends (they call it "privatization"), I see them pushing all of us, collectively, toward the brink of some sort of social Big Bang: the founder effect folks will have been pushed too far. If leaders were wise, they would see that large (make that huge!) blocks of raw, wild, untamed public lands serve as the greatest societal tranquilizer available. People, despite their flocking demeanor, cannot be crammed into ever decreasing spaces. I fear that we will all learn that lesson the hard way.

But this makes me think about *why* people connect with nature. There are those who view passionate expressions toward the woods as absurd. They proclaim that such "romantic" notions about nature are somehow less than acceptable behavior, which should not be considered seriously; that true and relevant thoughts on conservation (and preservation) can only take place within a framework of intellectual and philosophical discourse.

I am reminded of the story of two men who were discussing Christianity. One man was talking of commandments and dogma, quoting verses and comparing chapters, when suddenly the other man held up his hand. "What?" the first man asked. The second man shook his head, then said: "You have a son, don't you?" "Yes," said the first. "Well," the second man continued, "if I told you to go out and kill your son, would you?" "Of course not," said the first man. "Why not?" asked the second. "Because I love my son, that's why," the first man said. "Ah," the second man replied, "how strange you did not say it was because it is against the law." The first man was quiet. "You see," the second man continued, "that is the essence of Christianity. You do not act because of the law; you act because of love. It is that simple."

So it is with the woods. When one truly loves the woods, one does not need the crutch of intellectualism or philosophy to explain reasons for keeping it. And yet, we seem prone (or perhaps forced) to reduce all things to some empirical value. We sit uneasy if we cannot explain our reasons, as if we have to produce some sort of excuse, for leaving nature alone.

Only a fool would try to intellectualize the feelings of romance, or the love for one's child, or the reasons why we mourn. We do those things simply because we are human. So it is with nature. If we genuinely connect with the woods, the mountains, the prairies, the rivers, lakes, and streams, then we have connected emotionally, and not intellectually. That is a weld that can never be broken.

And therein rests the only valid answer to saving the environment: We must provide genuine access to it. But again, let me qualify that statement. Driving through a national park with the windows rolled up, the stereo playing, and the air conditioner on is *not* a genuine experience. People who only see mountains, forests, and deserts this way have never tasted nature in the true emotional and physical sense. They have given themselves, instead, a counterfeit sensation. This is merely indulging in more television, only this time the living room is the inside of a car, and the picture tube lies just beyond the windshield.

But then, this has become the norm. If people can't have a road (a *paved* road) into a patch of woods, if they can't have a nice motel waiting for them when they arrive, if they can't have a fancy restaurant nearby, then they tend to perceive the entire experience in a negative way. Could it be that modern men and women are just so incredibly soft they can no longer survive in the natural world? Perhaps history will record—if there is anyone around to record it—that *Homo sapiens sapiens* went the way of *Homo sapiens neanderthalensis,* but for paradoxical reasons. The Neandertals could not proceed past the rugged niche they had evolved to fill. Likewise we have become locked, in quite the opposite way, into fragile parameters from which divestment would seem impossible. But then, what better circumstances for the founder effect to occur? Those who *need* wilderness, and who are left with wilderness, will be the ones to inherit wilderness; though it might be said that the wilderness of the future will be void of things like trees and fresh water.

Not long ago a student said to me: "What is it with you? Do you want us all to go back to cave man days?" To which I answered: "That is precisely what I am trying to avoid."

And yet how can this be done? I submit that the answer lies in education, though not necessarily in traditional education. We must allow people to walk—mentally as well as physically—back into the woods. We must allow people to fuse with nature. We must provide places where people can savor utterly quiet, overpoweringly starry nights, total isolation, unmolested and unmediated *monte verde,* as it is, with nothing virtual about it. And let me make this perfectly clear: Real nature is *not* managed nature. Keep out those who insist on attaching radio collars to every poor creature that walks by. Keep out those who want to census every plant in the area. Keep out those who demand that transects and grids crisscross the territory with bright colored ribbons, strings, tags and what not. KEEP OUT THE MANAGERS! Let them go somewhere else, so they can turn wilderness into a park—though they won't understand that that is exactly what they are doing.

And then, when you finally walk through an area where no cars or bikes or even horses are allowed, you should accompany each step with a prayer, because this is the closest that you will ever come to knowing God; He, after all, created a garden in the beginning. Pray and be reverent; to destroy nature is nothing short of blasphemy.

We may already have gone too far with our greed and destruction. Still, I must remain hopeful. I tell my students who plan to become elementary school teachers that they are the most important people in my class. "You," I tell them, "must show the children the woods. Show them the animals, and the birds and plants. Start them out young, and they will know what to do."

That is the way it was for me. I was lucky, I guess. I had people in my life who were willing to share their love for the Brushlands. I have done the same with my sons. Someday, when I am an old man, I hope to have a grandson to walk with, as I walked with Papagrande. I will point out a deer track, and the tracks of coyotes, bobcats, skunks, armadillos, javelina, and all the other creatures of the brush. We will pause and collect cenizo leaves, and we will brew them into a delicious tea back at camp. We will munch on the sweet "chilis" of biznaga de chilitos. We will pick some ripe ebony pods in order to roast the beans over hot coals. We will snack on the berries of a coma. We will not go hungry. And then perhaps my grandson will look up at me and say, "Gee, you sure know a lot about the woods. How did you learn all of this neat stuff?" I suspect that before I answer, I will pause, remembering another young fellow who walked the sleeping woods long ago, and another old man who was asked the same questions. Perhaps then, I'll understand in the most profound way why Papagrande sometimes hesitated before he answered me—and why he'd look off at the clouds and smile. I guess he, too, was thinking of still another young boy who lived in the Brushlands once upon a time.

Notes

PART II. THE DARK YEARS

1. Rootplows are generally dragged behind a bulldozer. The plow, consisting of a row of steel teeth, digs into the ground and literally shreds the plant's roots.
2. A concise history of deep South Texas can be found in David Montejano's book, *Anglos and Mexicans in the Making of Texas: 1836–1986* (Austin: University of Texas Press, 1987).
3. M. Salinas, *Indians of the Rio Grande Delta* (Austin: University of Texas Press, 1990).
4. On page 11, in addition to Hidalgo, Cameron, and Willacy counties, Salinas adds the Mexican municipalities of Matamoros, Valle Hermoso, Rio Bravo, and Reynosa, all in the state of Tamaulipas.
5. Salinas 1990:128. It should be noted also that the Indians of the Rio Grande Delta region sometimes employed canoes as a means of transportation along the Rio Grande as well as through the resacas, swamps, and tributaries.
6. Salinas 1990:132.
7. By the time of Prohibition, a concerted effort by farmers had begun to destroy the dense woodlands that occupied Cameron and Willacy counties.

PART III. FIGHTING BACK

1. "U.S. Officials: Fraud in Crop Insurance Rife," *McAllen Monitor*, February 22, 1996.
2. I have used the term anthropocentrism as defined by J. B. Callicott, who says that "in Western religious and philosophical tradition, only human beings are worthy of ethical consideration, [and] that all things are regarded as mere means to human ends." J. B. Callicott, "Conversation, Values, and Ethics," in G. K. Meffe and C. R. Carroll (eds.), *Principles of Conservation Biology* (Sunderland, Mass.: Sinauer Associates, 1994), pp. 24–29.
3. Environmental educators have made clear distinctions between what should be called environmental "problems" and environmental "issues." For example, pollution in the Rio Grande is an environmental problem. Water pollution in general is an environmental issue.
4. The terms *biocentric* and *biocentrism* have generally been defined as a self-awareness that humankind does not stand at the center of the bioshpere, nor is the biosphere merely an object to be exploited ad hoc. On the contrary, people occupy a position relative to all other living things.
5. A. Leopold, *A Sand County Almanac* (Oxford: Oxford University Press, 1949);

D. Foreman, *Confessions of an Eco-Warrior* (New York: Crown Publishers, 1991).

6. D. D. Chiras, *Environmental Science: Action for a Sustainable Future,* 4th ed. (Redwood City, Calif.: Benjamin-Cummings Publishing Company, 1994). Chiras, like other environmental scientists, deplores the "frontier [Western] ethic" of solving problems by simply calling upon scientists to "fix it." He points out that America, like other developed countries, is a "low-synergy society." Such societies seek answers to environmental problems by finding ways to get around obstacles without addressing the underlying conditions that have created those obstacles.
7. In principle, the founder effect states that new species can derive from sudden implosions of the gene pool, usually brought on by geographic isolation or by an environmental trauma that causes a drastic reduction in the availability of transferrable genetic information. I envision here, however, a founder effect based not on some extrinsic catalyst but rather on an intrinsic psychic change, expressed in behaviors that run contrary to cultural norms but that at the same time prove to be selectively advantageous.

Printed in the USA
CPSIA information can be obtained
at www.ICGtesting.com
JSHW021241151123
51837JS00002B/14

9 781623 494865